THE GREAT CAT

POEMS ABOUT CATS

••••••••••••••••••

SELECTED AND EDITED BY
EMILY FRAGOS

EVERYMAN'S LIBRARY
POCKET POETS

Alfred A. Knopf   New York London Toronto

THIS IS A BORZOI BOOK
PUBLISHED BY ALFRED A. KNOPF

This selection by Emily Fragos first published in
Everyman's Library, 2005
Copyright © 2005 by Everyman's Library

A list of acknowledgments to copyright owners appears at the back
of this volume.

All rights reserved under International and Pan-American Copyright
Conventions. Published in the United States by Alfred A. Knopf,
a division of Random House, Inc., New York, and simultaneously in
Canada by Random House of Canada Limited, Toronto. Distributed
by Random House, Inc., New York. Published in the United Kingdom
by Everyman's Library, Northburgh House, 10 Northburgh Street,
London EC1V 0AT. Distributed by Random House (UK) Ltd.

US website: www.randomhouse.com/everymans

ISBN 1-4000-4334-4 (US)
1-84159-764-3 (UK)

A CIP catalogue record for this book is available from the British Library

Typography by Peter B. Willberg
Typeset in the UK by AccComputing, North Barrow, Somerset
Printed and bound in Germany by GGP Media GmbH, Pössneck

CONTENTS

MYSTERY

THE SUPERIOR CAT

CAT ANTICS

THE AMOROUS CAT

SLEEPING, DREAMING

11

FOREWORD

Here they are: Hodge, Jeoffry, Pangur Bán, the Cats of Baudelaire, Yeats's Minnaloushe, and the cats from Mother Goose and Dr Seuss. While collecting material for this anthology I encountered such an abundance of glorious poems from across the centuries and continents that I was overwhelmed by sheer beauty, mystery, sagacity, dancing, and dreaming. I was overwhelmed, too, by humankind's enduring fascination and adoration for the Great Cat, evidence of which dates back as far as the tomb walls of Thebes three thousand years ago.

Apart from the poems and quotations you will discover in these pages, some familiar and others new and surprising in their voice and variety, I discovered many enchantments I could not find room to include, such as these lines from Tennyson's *The Holy Grail*: 'I will be deafer than the blue-eyed cat,/And thrice as blind as any noon-tide owl,/To holy virgins in their ecstasies,/Henceforward.' Richard Brathwaite's sixteenth-century *Barnabee's Journal* opens with the powerfully cadenced and scarily evocative lines: 'To Banbury came I, O profane one!/Where I saw a Puritane-one/Hanging of his cat on Monday/For killing of a mouse on Sunday.' On a happier note, I learned that *The Cat's Fugue*, a piece by Domenico Scarlatti, came into being when his playful kitten ran

13

up the harpsichord keys and composed the first three bars. Scarlatti, inspired, did the rest.

The poems I have included here are organized by the creatures' attributes and actions, but also by their relationships to other animals, and, most profoundly, to us.

William Shakespeare's allusions to the cat are many, but for this volume I chose the hypnotic cat before the mouse's hole, from *Pericles*, for its intense compression and imagery. There are endless poems about the relationship of cat to mouse, some showing pity for the little mouse and some understanding of the cat's nature. And what to say about birds, those free, winged creatures ever fleeing from the cat's grasp? Are you a cat person or a dog person? As this collection shows, poets have been considering that question, sometimes comically, for centuries.

Long before the idea of therapy animals came into play, poets extolled the benefits of a cat at one's side and the unexpected, unbearable anguish of losing the animal who has become the 'soul of the house,' as Jean Cocteau put it. It is not only cats who do the leaving: the Sufi master Hafiz worries about abandoning his mystical cat in 'Who will feed my cat?' Fernando Pessoa, inhabiting multiple personae, is envious of the singular cat tumbling freely down the street. Cesare Pavese's secret despair is fathomed only by the mysteriously empathetic creatures in a haunting refrain, 'the cats will know.'

Can there be a poetic masterpiece more reverential than Christopher Smart's 'My Cat Jeoffry,' from *Jubilate Agno*, written from Bedlam in 1760? Like all his brother and sister cats, the electrifying Jeoffry 'is a mixture of gravity and waggery,' and 'every house is incomplete without him and a blessing is lacking in the spirit.' Smart's poem, included here in its entirety, does not reach a conclusion in its unfettered joy, awe, and devotion, but merely comes to an abrupt stop, as this book must come to a stop, launching us into new rounds of introspection and honor for the Great Cat.

EMILY FRAGOS

ADORATION

'What greater gift than the love of a cat.'

CHARLES DICKENS

From THE SEVENTY-FIVE PRAISES OF RA
inscribed on the walls of royal tombs of Thebes in Egypt
(c. 1200–1100 B.C.E.)

Praise be to thee, O Ra, exalted Sekhem,
thou art the Great Cat, the avenger of the gods
and the judge of words and the president of
the sovereign chiefs and the governor of the
holy Circle; thou art indeed the bodies of the
Great Cat.

CHANG TUAN'S CATS

Scholar Chang Tuan was fond of cats,
And had seven of them,
Wonderful beasts with wonderful names.
They were:
    Guardian of the East
    White Phoenix
    Purple Blossom
    Drive-Away-Vexation
    Brocade Sash
    Cloud Pattern
    Ten Thousand Strings of Cash
Each was worth several pieces of gold,
And nothing could persuade Chang
To part with them.

TR. FELICITY BAST
AFTER WANG CHIH (*c.* 1100 C.E.)

CAT

As if he owned the place, a cat
    meanders through my mind,
sleek and proud, yet so discreet
    in making known his will

that I hear music when he mews,
    and even when he purrs
a tender timbre in the sound
    compels my consciousness –

a secret rhythm penetrates
    to unsuspected depths,
obsessive as a line of verse
    and potent as a drug:

all woes are spirited away,
    I hear ecstatic news –
it seems a telling language has
    no need of words at all.

My heart, assenting instrument,
    is masterfully played;
no other bow across its strings
    can draw such music out

the way this cat's uncanny voice
    – seraphic, alien –
can reconcile discordant strains
    into close harmony!

One night his brindled fur gave off
    a perfume so intense
I seemed to be embalmed because
    (just once!) I fondled him …

Familiar spirit, genius, judge,
    the cat presides – inspires
events that he appears to spurn,
    half goblin and half god!

and when my spellbound eyes at last
    relinquish worship of
this cat they love to contemplate
    and look inside myself,

I find to my astonishment
    like living opals there
his fiery pupils, embers which
    observe me fixedly.

CHARLES BAUDELAIRE
TR. RICHARD HOWARD

From JUBILATE AGNO
(*A Poem from Bedlam*)

For I will consider my cat Jeoffry.

For he is the servant of the living God, duly and daily
serving him.

For at the first glance of the glory of God in the East
he worships in his way.

For this is done by wreathing his body seven times
round with elegant quickness.

For when he leaps up to catch the musk, which is the
blessing of God upon his prayer.

For he rolls upon prank to work it in.

For having done duty and received blessing he begins
to consider himself.

For this he performs in ten degrees.

For first he looks upon his fore-paws to see
if they are clean.

For secondly he kicks up behind to clear away there.

For thirdly he works it upon stretch with
the fore-paws extended.

For fourthly he sharpens his paws by wood.

For fifthly he washes himself.

For sixthly he rolls upon wash.

For seventhly he fleas himself, that he may not be
interrupted upon the beat.

For eighthly he rubs himself against a post.

For ninthly he looks up for his instructions.

For tenthly he goes in quest of food.

For having consider'd God and himself he will
consider his neighbour.

For if he meets another cat he will kiss her
in kindness.

For when he takes his prey he plays with it to give it
[a] chance.

For one mouse in seven escapes by his dallying.

For when his day's work is done his business more
properly begins.

For he keeps the Lord's watch in the night against
the adversary.

For he counteracts the powers of darkness by his
electrical skin and glaring eyes.

For he counteracts the Devil, who is death, by
brisking about the life.

For in his morning orisons he loves the sun and the
sun loves him.

For he is of the tribe of Tiger.

For the Cherub Cat is a term of the Angel Tiger.

For he has the subtlety and hissing of a serpent, which
in goodness he suppresses.

For he will not do destruction, if he is well-fed, neither
will he spit without provocation.

For he purrs in thankfulness, when God tells him he's
a good Cat.

For he is an instrument for the children to learn
      benevolence upon.
For every house is incompleat without him &
      a blessing is lacking in the Spirit.
For the Lord commanded Moses concerning the cats
      at the departure of the Children of Israel
      from Egypt.
For every family had one cat at least in the bag.
For the English cats are the best in Europe.
For he is the cleanest in the use of his fore-paws
      of any quadrupeds.
For the dexterity of his defence is an instance of the
      love of God to him exceedingly.
For he is the quickest to his mark of any creature.
For he is tenacious of his point.
For he is a mixture of gravity and waggery.
For he knows that God is his Saviour.
For there is nothing sweeter than his peace when at rest.
For there is nothing brisker than his life
      when in motion.
For he is of the Lord's poor and so indeed is he called
      by benevolence perpetually – Poor Jeoffry!
      poor Jeoffry! the rat has bit thy throat.
For I bless the name of the Lord Jesus that Jeoffry
      is better.
For the divine spirit comes about his body to sustain it
      in compleat cat.

For his tongue is exceeding pure so that it has in
  purity what it wants in musick.
For he is docile and can learn certain things.
For he can set up with gravity which is patience
  upon approbation.
For he can fetch and carry, which is patience
  in employment.
For he can jump over a stick which is patience upon
  proof positive.
For he can spraggle upon waggle at the word of
  command.
For he can jump from an eminence into his
  master's bosom.
For he can catch the cork and toss it again.
For he is hated by the hypocrite and miser.
For the former is afraid of detection.
For the latter refuses the charge.
For he camels his back to bear the first motion
  of business.
For he is good to think on, if a man would express
  himself neatly.
For he made a great figure in Egypt for his
  signal services.
For he killed the Icneumon-rat very pernicious by land.
For his ears are so acute that they sting again.
For from this proceeds the passing quickness of
  his attention.

For by stroaking of him I have found out electricity.
For I perceived God's light about him both wax
and fire.
For the Electrical fire is the spiritual substance, which
God sends from heaven to sustain the bodies
both of man and beast.
For God has blessed him in the variety of his
movements.
For, tho he cannot fly, he is an excellent clamberer.
For his motions upon the face of the earth are more
than any other quadrupeds.
For he can tread to all the measures upon the musick.
For he can swim for life.
For he can creep.

HODGE, THE CAT

Burly and big, his books among,
    Good Samuel Johnson sat,
With frowning brows and wig askew,
His snuff-strewn waistcoat far from new;
So stern and menacing his air,
   That neither Black Sam, nor the maid
To knock or interrupt him dare;
    Yet close beside him, unafraid,
      Sat Hodge, the cat.

'This participle,' the Doctor wrote,
    'The modern scholar cavils at,
But,' – even as he penned the word,
A soft, protesting note was heard;
The Doctor fumbled with his pen,
   The dawning thought took wings and flew,
The sound repeated, come again,
   It was a faint, reminding 'Mew!'
      From Hodge, the cat.

'Poor Pussy!' said the learned man,
    Giving the glossy fur a pat,
'It is your dinner time, I know,
And – well, perhaps I ought to go;
For if Sam every day were sent

Off from his work your fish to buy,
Why, men are men, he might resent,
    And starve or kick you on the sly;
        Eh! Hodge, my cat?'

The Dictionary was laid down,
    The Doctor tied his vast cravat,
And down the buzzing street he strode,
Taking an often-trodden road,
And halted at a well-known stall:
    'Fishmonger,' spoke the Doctor gruff,
'Give me six oysters, that is all;
    Hodge knows when he has had enough,
        Hodge is my cat.'

Then home; puss dined, and while in sleep
    He chased a visionary rat,
His master sat him down again,
Rewrote his page, renibbed his pen;
Each 'i' was dotted, each 't' was crossed,
    He labored on for all to read,
Nor deemed that time was waste or lost
    Spent in supplying the small need
        Of Hodge, the cat.

The dear old Doctor! fierce of mien,
    Untidy, arbitrary, fat,
What gentle thought his name enfold!
So generous of his scanty gold.
So quick to love, so hot to scorn,
   Kind to all sufferers under heaven,
A tend'rer despot ne'er was born;
    His big heart held a corner, even
      For Hodge, the cat.

   (SUSAN COOLIDGE)

A LION IN WINTER
for William, my Blue Maine Coon

As long as the lions are rampant, I will stay
With him.
                As long as the clouded leopards

Surround the clouded bed with their gold & cirrus
Air, I will be there too. I was reading

When the winter shooed-
Away the fall and whitely lit the oil lamps of early

Dark. The night was turret-shaped in childhood,
                A bunch of mint and mane and swale.

What will I be when he is husk
To himself,
                Some flax or ghost of lynx in later winter light.

BEAUTY

'The smallest feline is a masterpiece.'

LEONARDO DA VINCI

WHITE CATS
To Albert Dugrip

In the clear gold of sunlight, stretching their backs,
– White as snow – see the voluptuous cats,
Closing eyes jealous of their inner glooms,
Slumbering in the tepid warmth of their illumined fur.

Their coats have the dazzle of dawn-bathed glaciers.
Inside them, their bodies, frail, sinewy, and slender,
Feel the shiverings of a girl inside her dress,
And their beauty refines itself in endless languors.

No question but their Soul of old has animated
The flesh of a philosopher, or a woman's body,
For since then their dazzling and inestimable
     whiteness

Holding the mingled splendor of a grand premiere,
Ennobles them to a rank of calm contempt,
Indifferent to everything but *Light* itself!

From THE DIVAN-I KABIR

Rosebuds
Surrounded by thorns:
Mother cat carrying babies in mouth.

JALALUDDIN RUMI
TR. LIZ WAYGOOD

THE SPRING IS A CAT

On a cat's fur soft as pollen,
The mild Spring's fragrance lingers.

In a cat's eyes round as golden bells,
The mad Spring's flame glows.

On a cat's gently closed lips,
The soft Spring's drowsiness lies.

On a cat's sharp whiskers,
The green Spring's life dances.

JANG-HI LEE
TR. CHANG-SOO KOH

THE CAT SHOW

Fastidious judges with dainty hands
disinfect tables; disease must not be spread.
The cats await examination, bred
for showing, their coats caressed and muzzles scanned
for perfect proportion, roundness, balance, brands.
Oblivious and docile Persians are led
from cages: ribboned, groomed, prudently fed.
One judge tries to trick them, flicking peacock strands.
The crowd feels shabby, awed by nature's ways:
the finish, fullness, panache and drapery;
massive and slender, peaked or pug bodies;
refined intelligence, lioness be praised.
The priestess cat is held on high – sacred.
This contest claims victory for gifts from God.

WHITE CAT BLUES

The white cat with sapphire eyes
can't be colour blind
must see the world
                           as blue.
Blue horses, blue light spilling
from the window, blue willows,
blue women
carrying bowls of bluish cream.

        How beautiful I feel
all blue – shoulders, feet and hair,
the brilliant air,
blue wind
            touching everything.

Tonight desire
                    the distance
between the moon and the white cat
sleeping under the apple tree
                    (the apples cold and blue)
will be the precise colour
of the cat's dreams of rain.

WITHOUT VIOLENCE

That cat who comes during sleep, quiet
On his cushioned claws, without violence,
Who enters the house with a low warm rattle
In his throat; that cat who has been said
To crawl into a baby's crib without brushing
The bars, to knit his paws on the pale
Flannel of the infant's nightdress, to settle
In sleep chin to chin with the dear one
And softly steal the child's breath
Without malice, as easily as pulling
A silk scarf completely through a gold ring;

The same cat who has been known to nudge
Through castle doors, to part tent flaps,
To creep to the breasts of brave men,
Ease between their blankets, to stretch
Full length on the satin bodices of lovely
Women, to nuzzle their cheeks with his great
Feline mane; it was that cat who leaped last night
Through the west window of father's bedroom,
Who chose to knead his night's rest on my father's
Shoulder, who slept well, breathing deeply,
Leaving just before dawn to saunter toward
The north, his magnificent tail and rump
Swaying with a listless and gorgeous grace.

PATTIANN ROGERS   39

THE SINGING CAT

It was a little captive cat
    Upon a crowded train
His mistress takes him from his box
    To ease his fretful pain.

She holds him tight upon her knee
    The graceful animal
And all the people look at him
    He is so beautiful.

But oh he pricks and oh he prods
    And turns upon her knee
Then lifteth up his innocent voice
    In plaintive melody.

He lifteth up his innocent voice
    He lifteth up, he singeth
And to each human countenance
    A smile of grace he bringeth.

He lifteth up his innocent paw
　　Upon her breast he clingeth
And everybody cries, Behold
　　The cat, the cat that singeth.

He lifteth up his innocent voice
　　He lifteth up, he singeth
And all the people warm themselves
　　In the love his beauty bringeth.

AT THE GRAVE OF ELIZABETH BISHOP

I, detaching myself from the human I, Henri,
without thick eyeglasses or rubberized white skin,
stretched out like a sinewy cat in the brown grass
to see what I felt, wrapping my tail around me,
hiding my eyes.
              I slept. I waited. I sucked air,
instead of milk. I listened to pigeons murmuring.
Scratching my ear, I couldn't tell if I was male
    or female.
The bundled energy of my life drifted along
somewhere between pain and pleasure,
until a deerfly launched an attack
and anger, like a florist's scissors,
pinched the bright chrysanthemum of my brain.
Overhead, the long enfolding branches,
weighted down with Venetian green,
suffused the air with possibility.
I felt like a realist, recovering from style.
Grief and dignity swirled around discreetly,
transferring to me an aura of calm,
as I lay in a shawl of gold light,
licking my paws, licking my throat,
my smooth imperturbable face revealing nothing,
even when I thought about my first loves,
surface and symbol, rubbing against me,

humping in the shadows, making my whole
    body tremble.
I purred, watching an iridescent blue beetle
imbibe chlorophyll from a leaf.
I flared my nostrils, hearing a starling
splash in an amphora of rainwater.
With my paws in the air, exposing my ripe belly,
I rubbed my spine, a little drunk on the ultraviolet rays
and on myself, I confess.
Then the sky cleared. Birds were flying.
I felt a deep throbbing, as from a distant factory,
binding me to others, a faint battering of wings
    against glass
that was the heart in the lovely dark behind my breast,
as I was crouching to tie my shoelaces,
feeling strange in the meaty halves of my buttocks,
until I sprinkled a little earth on my head,
like Hadrian reunited with the place he loved.

THE TYGER

Tyger! Tyger! burning bright
In the forests of the night,
What immortal hand or eye
Could frame thy fearful symmetry?

In what distant deeps or skies
Burnt the fire of thine eyes?
On what wings dare he aspire?
What the hand dare seize the fire?

And what shoulder, & what art,
Could twist the sinews of thy heart?
And when thy heart began to beat,
What dread hand? & what dread feet?

What the hammer, what the chain?
In what furnace was thy brain?
What the anvil, what dread grasp
Dare its deadly terrors clasp?

When the stars threw down their spears,
And water'd heaven with their tears,
Did he smile his work to see?
Did he who made the Lamb make thee?

Tyger! Tyger! burning bright
In the forests of the night,
What immortal hand or eye
Dare frame thy fearful symmetry?

THE CAT'S EYE

In the eyes of the cat
Is the color of the sea,
On a sunny day, in winter.

YORIE
TR. TZE-SI HUANG

THE CAT

Flourishing his head around
He licks himself smooth and sleek –
The moonlight cat!

KUSTATAO
TR. TZE-SI HUANG

'ULTRA-PINK PEONY'

Ultra-pink peony …
Silver Siamese soft cat …
Gold-dust butterfly …

BUSON
TR. PETER BEILENSON

MYSTERY

'I wish I could write as mysterious as a cat.'

EDGAR ALLAN POE

BLACK CAT

A ghost, though invisible, still is like a place
your sight can knock on, echoing; but here
within this thick black pelt, your strongest gaze
will be absorbed and utterly disappear:

just as a raving madman, when nothing else
can ease him, charges into his dark night
howling, pounds on the padded wall, and feels
the rage being taken in and pacified.

She seems to hide all looks that have ever fallen
into her, so that, like an audience,
she can look them over, menacing and sullen,
and curl to sleep with them. But all at once

as if awakened, she turns her face to yours;
and with a shock, you see yourself, tiny,
inside the golden amber of her eyeballs
suspended, like a prehistoric fly.

RAINER MARIA RILKE
TR. STEPHEN MITCHELL

TO A CAT

Mirrors are not more wrapt in silences
nor the arriving dawn more secretive;
you, in the moonlight, are that panther figure
which we can only spy at from a distance.
By the mysterious functioning of some
divine decree, we seek you out in vain;
remoter than the Ganges or the sunset,
yours is the solitude, yours is the secret.
Your back allows the tentative caress
my hand extends. And you have condescended,
since that eternity, by now forgotten,
to take love from a flattering human hand.
You live in other time, lord of your realm –
a world as closed and separate as dream.

THE CATS WILL KNOW

Still the rain will fall
on your sweet cobble pavements,
a rain light
as a breath or a step.
Still the breeze and sunrise
will flower lightly
beneath your step
when you come in again.
Among the flowers and sills
the cats will know.

There will be other days,
there will be other voices.
You will smile by yourself.
The cats will know.
Old, old words you will hear,
weary and vain
like the costumes cast aside
from yesterday's revels.
You too will make gestures.
You will answer words –
visage of spring –
you too will make gestures.

The cats will know,
visage of spring;
the light rain
and dawn the color of hyacinth,
that tear the heart
of one who hopes for you no longer,
are the sad smile
you smile by yourself.
There will be other days,
other voices and awakening.
We will suffer in the sunrise,
visage of spring.

THE CAT

The cat
    licks its paw and
lies down in
    the bookshelf nook
                She
        can lie in a
        sphinx position
without moving for so
        many hours
and then turn her head
    to me and
        rise and stretch
and turn
        her back to me and
    lick her paw again as if
no real time had passed
    It hasn't
        and she is the sphinx with
    all the time in the world
        in the desert of her time
The cat
    knows where flies die
      sees ghosts in motes of air
        and shadows in sunbeams

She hears
        the music of the spheres and
the hum in the wires of houses
        and the hum of the universe
in interstellar spaces
        but
prefers domestic places
        and the hum of the heater

THE RABBIT AS KING OF THE GHOSTS

The difficulty to think at the end of day,
When the shapeless shadow covers the sun
And nothing is left except light on your fur –

There was the cat slopping its milk all day,
Fat cat, red tongue, green mind, white milk
And August the most peaceful month.

To be, in the grass, in the peacefullest time,
Without that monument of cat,
The cat forgotten in the moon;

And to feel that the light is a rabbit-light,
In which everything is meant for you
And nothing need be explained;

Then there is nothing to think of. It comes of itself;
And east rushes west and west rushes down,
No matter. The grass is full

And full of yourself. The trees around are for you,
The whole of the wideness of night is for you,
A self that touches all edges,

You become a self that fills the four corners of night.
The red cat hides away in the fur-light
And there you are humped high, humped up,

You are humped higher and higher, black as stone –
You sit with your head like a carving in space
And the little green cat is a bug in the grass.

THE THING ABOUT CATS

Cats hang out with witches quite a lot;
that's not it.

The thing about cats is
they're always looking at you.
Especially when you're asleep.

Some cats pretend they're not looking
until you're not looking.
They are not to be trusted.

Some cats scowl because they're wearing
imitation fur. They feel inferior.

Some other cats look at you straight on
so that you can't drink your drink
or make love
                but keep thinking
that cat's looking at me straight on.

But all cats do the same:
they look at you
                    and you look out
and in.

A cat is not a conscience; I'm not
saying that.

What I'm saying is
                    why are they looking?

CAT

Dear creature by the fire a-purr,
    Strange idol, eminently bland,
Miraculous puss! As o'er your fur
    I trail a negligible hand,

And gaze into your gazing eyes,
    And wonder in a demi-dream,
What mystery it is that lies,
    Behind those slits that glare and gleam,

An exquisite enchantment falls
    About the portals of my sense;
Meandering through enormous halls,
    I breathe luxurious frankincense,

An ampler air, a warmer June
    Enfold me, and my wondering eye
Salutes a more imperial moon
    Throned in a more resplendent sky

Than ever knew this northern shore.
    Oh, strange! For you are with me too,
And I who am a cat once more
    Follow the woman that was you

With tail erect and pompous march,
　　The proudest puss that ever trod,
Through many a grove, 'neath many an arch,
　　Impenetrable as a god.

Down many an alabaster flight
　　Of broad and cedar-shaded stairs,
While over us the elaborate night
　　Mysteriously gleams and glares.

THE PANTHER

His vision, from the constantly passing bars,
has grown so weary that it cannot hold
anything else. It seems to him there are
a thousand bars; and behind the bars, no world.

As he paces in cramped circles, over and over,
the movement of his powerful soft strides
is like a ritual dance around a center
in which a mighty will stands paralyzed.

Only at times, the curtain of the pupils
lifts, quietly – . An image enters in,
rushes down through the tensed, arrested muscles,
plunges into the heart and is gone.

RAINER MARIA RILKE
TR. STEPHEN MITCHELL

THE SPHINX

In a dim corner of my room for longer than my
    fancy thinks,
A beautiful and silent Sphinx has watched me through
    the shifting gloom.

Inviolate and immobile she does not rise, she does
    not stir
For silver moons are naught to her and naught to her
    the suns that reel.

Red follows grey across the air, the waves of
    moonlight ebb and flow,
But with the Dawn she does not go and in the
    night-time she is there.

Dawn follows Dawn and Nights grow old and all the
    while this curious cat
Lies crouching on the Chinese mat with eyes of satin
    rimmed with gold.

Upon the mat she lies and leers and on the tawny
    throat of her
Flutters the soft and silky fur ripples to her
    pointed ears.

Come forth, my lovely seneschal! so somnolent,
    so statuesque!
Come forth you exquisite grotesque! half woman and
    half animal!

Come forth my lovely languorous Sphinx! and put
    your head upon my knee!
And let me stroke your throat and see your body
    spotted like the Lynx!

And let me touch those curving claws of yellow ivory,
    and grasp
The tail that like a monstrous Asp coils round your
    heavy velvet paws!

OSCAR WILDE   63

THE SUPERIOR CAT

'I believe cats to be spirits come to earth.
A cat, I am sure, could walk on a cloud without
coming through.'

JULES VERNE

CAT SCAT

I am watching Cleo listening, our cat
listening to Mozart's *Magic Flute*. What
can she be hearing? What
can the air carry into her ears like that,
her ears swivelling like radio dishes that
are tuned to all the noise of the world, flat
and sharp, high and low, a scramble of this and that
she can decode like nobody's business, acrobat
of random airs as she is? Although of course a bat
is better at it, sifting out of its acoustic habitat
the sound of the very shape of things automat-
ically — and on the wing, at that. The *Magic Flute*! What
a joy it is, I feel, and wonder (to the end this little scat)
does, or can, the cat.

THE CATS OF GREECE

The cats of Greece have
eyes grey as plague.
Their voices are limpid,
all hunger.
As they dodge in the gutters
their bones clack.
Dogs run from them.
In tavernas they sit
at tableside and
watch you eat.
Their moonpale cries
hurl themselves
against your full spoon.
If you touch one gently
it goes crazy.
Its eyes turn up.
It wraps itself
around your ankle
and purrs a rusty millennium,
you liar,
you tourist.

THE CAT OF THE HOUSE

Over the hearth with my 'minishing eyes I muse
Until after
The last coal dies.
Every tunnel of the mouse,
Every channel of the cricket,
I have smelt.
I have felt
The secret shifting of the mouldered rafter,
And heard
Every bird in the thicket.
I see
You
Nightingale up in your tree!
I, born of a race of strange things,
Of deserts, great temples, great kings,
In the hot sands where the nightingale never sings!

THE VAIN CAT

Remarked a Tortoise to a Cat:
'Your speed's a thing to marvel at!
I saw you as you flitted by,
And wished I were one-half so spry.'
The Cat said, humbly: 'Why, indeed
I was not showing then my speed –
That was a poor performance.' Then
She said exultantly (as when
The condor feels his bosom thrill
Remembering Chimborazo's hill,
and how he soared so high above,
It looked a valley, he a dove):
''Twould fire your very carapace
To see me with a dog in chase!'
Its snout in any kind of swill,
Pride, like a pig, will suck its fill.

SISTERHOOD

There's a gray cat who's not allowed into the house
where our cat for twenty years has been the one cat.

There's a storm working over the low mountains,
building with a stillness of air and light

over the nearest peaks. And soon the rain,
the full storm gets under way, thunder and light,

the passing thickness of air, the sudden rush
of wind, and the sheet of rain spraying the valley.

The gray cat presses against the door frame, and we sit
down to dinner, our cat in the third chair, the stew

done right and placed on the table, the wine poured.
The evening survives the storm and we walk out
    for a look

at what's left. A moon finally free, a hostage
sprung from a Jihad of clouds breaking up.
    The wet grass

regains its starch from this afternoon's wet heat,
and the gray cat emerges from under the porch steps,

71

dry but intense, charging our legs and getting over
in the language of cats her wish to enter our lives.

In the window, mirroring the table lamp, our cat,
shrewd, disappointed, and accusatory, studies us.

She's hurt and shows no apparent sympathy for a sister
left to the cold of the outside world.
    We're not surprised,

she's an indoor cat, her claws clipped, her movements
suited to the angles of furniture, the surface of rugs.

She will stand before her bowl of food and demand
    our best,
a gourmet cat when hungry: squab, fillet, hearts
    of chicken.

From CAT

The animal kingdom came
faultily:
too wide in the rump or too
sad-headed.
Little by little they disposed
their proportions,
invented their landscape,
collected their graces and satellites, and took to the air.
Only the cat
issued
wholly a cat,
intact and vainglorious:
he came forth a consummate identity,
knew what he wanted, and walked tall.

Men wish they were fishes or birds;
the worm would be winged,
the dog is a dispossessed lion;
engineers would be poets;
flies ponder the swallow's prerogative
and pets impersonate flies –
but the cat
intends nothing but cat:
he is cat
from his tail to his chin whiskers:
from his living presumption of mouse
and the darkness, to the gold of his irises.

PABLO NERUDA   73
TR. BEN BELITT

'CAT, YOU TUMBLE
DOWN THE STREET'

Cat, you tumble down the street
As if it were your bed.
I think such luck's a treat,
Like feeding without being fed.

You're just a pawn in the hands
Of fate, as stones are, and people!
You follow your instinct and glands;
What you feel you feel – it's simple.

Because you're like that you're happy;
You're all the nothing you see.
I look at myself – it's not me.
I know myself – I'm not I.

TR. EDWIN HONIG AND SUSAN M. BROWN

THE CATS OF ST NICHOLAS

'That's the Cape of Cats ahead,' the captain said to me,
pointing through the mist to a low stretch of shore,
the beach deserted; it was Christmas Day –
'... and there, in the distance to the west, is where
     Aphrodite rose out of the waves;
they call the place "Greek's Rock."
Left ten degrees rudder!'
She had Salome's eyes, the cat I lost a year ago;
and old Ramazan, how he would look death square in
     the eyes,
whole days long in the snow of the East,
under the frozen sun,
days long square in the eyes: the young hearth god.
Don't stop, traveler.
'Left ten degrees rudder,' muttered the helmsman.

... my friend, though, might well have stopped short,
now between ships,
shut up in a small house with pictures,
searching for windows behind the frames.
The ship's bell struck
like a coin from some vanished city
that brings to mind, as it falls,
alms from another time.
'It's strange,' the captain said.

'That bell – given what day it is –
reminded me of another one, the monastery bell.
A monk told me the story,
a half-mad monk, a kind of dreamer.

'It was during the great drought,
forty years without rain,
the whole island devastated,
people dying and snakes giving birth.
This cape had millions of snakes
fat as a man's leg
and full of poison.
In those days the monastery of St Nicholas
was held by the monks of St Basil,
and they couldn't go out to work their fields,
couldn't put their flocks to pasture.
In the end they were saved by the cats they raised.
Every day at dawn a bell would strike
and an army of cats would move into battle.
They'd fight the day long,
until the bell sounded for the evening feed.
Supper done, the bell would sound again
and they'd go to battle through the night.
They say it was a marvellous sight to see them,
some lame, some blind, others missing
a nose, an ear, their hides in shreds.

So to the sound of four bells a day
months went by, years, season after season.
Wildly obstinate, always wounded,
they annihilated the snakes; but in the end they
　　disappeared;
they just couldn't take in that much poison.
Like a sunken ship
they left no trace on the surface:
not a meow, not even a bell.
Steady as you go!
Poor devils, what could they do,
fighting like that day and night, drinking
the poisonous blood of those snakes?
Generations of poison, centuries of poison.'
'Steady as you go,' indifferently echoed the helmsman.

MAGIC CATS

(With acknowledgments to Susan Musgrave, whose
'Strawberry' poems started it all)

Most cats, with the exception of Burmese, do not
celebrate their birthdays. Rather, they are extremely
sentimental about Palm Sunday and Labour Day, at
which times they survive solely on white lace and
baloney sandwiches.

Cats on the whole are loath to discuss God.

Generally speaking, cats have no money, although
some of them secretly collect rare and valuable coins.

Cats believe that all human beings, animals and plants
should congregate in a huge heap in the centre of the
universe and promptly fall asleep together.

Of all the cats I have known, the ones I remember
most are: Bumble Bee, Buttonhole, Chocolate Bar,
Molten Lava and Mushroom. I also remember Tabby
who was sane as a star and spent all his time lying on
his back in the sink, thinking up appropriate names
for me.

Cats see their Keepers as massive phantoms, givers of
names and the excellent gravy of their days.

Cats who have been robbed of balls and claws do not lament. They become their Keeper's keepers.

When cats are hosts to fleas they assume the fleas are guests.

Most cats would rather be covered with live fleas than dead ones.

Cats hold no grudges and have no future. They invade nets of strangers with their eyes.

The patron saint of cats is called: Beast of the Skies, Warm Presence, Eyes.

Cats do not worry about the gurgling horrors of the disease listed in catbooks, some of which are Hairballs Enteritis and Bronchitis. But they do become very upset about Symptoms, which is the worst disease of all.

When cats grow listless (i.e. lose their list) they cease to entertain fleas. They mumble darkly about radishes and death. They listen to Beethoven and become overly involved in Medieval History.

When cats decide to die   they lie alone   lost among leaves beneath the dark winds and broad thunders of the world and pray to the Beast of the Skies, Warm, Presence, Eyes.

Broadly speaking, cats do not read Gothic novels, although they tend to browse through Mary Shelley on the day before Christmas.

The only reason cats do not carry passports is because they have no pockets.

When a black cat crosses your path it usually means that he is trying to get to the other side of the street.

Cats never get baptized. They lose their dry.

Cats only perspire during Lent.

Cats have no memory and no future. They are highly allergic to Prime Ministers, radishes, monks, poets, and death.

CAT ANTICS

'Balanchine trained his cat to perform brilliant jetés and tours en l'air. He says that at last he has a body worth choreographing for.'

BERNARD TAPER

THE CAT AND THE MOON

The cat went here and there
And the moon spun round like a top,
And the nearest kin of the moon,
The creeping cat, looked up.
Black Minnaloushe stared at the moon,
For, wander and wail as he would,
The pure cold light in the sky
Troubled his animal blood.
Minnaloushe runs in the grass
Lifting his delicate feet.
Do you dance, Minnaloushe, do you dance?
When two close kindred meet,
What better than call a dance?
Maybe the moon may learn,
Tired of that courtly fashion,
A new dance turn.
Minnaloushe creeps through the grass
From moonlit place to place,
The sacred moon overhead
Has taken a new phase.
Does Minnaloushe know that his pupils
Will pass from change to change,
And that from round to crescent,
From crescent to round they range?

Minnaloushe creeps through the grass
Alone, important and wise,
And lifts to the changing moon
His changing eyes.

EVERY CAT HAD A STORY

The yellow one from the bakery
smelled like a cream puff —
she followed us home.
We buried our faces
in her sweet fur.
One cat hid her head
while I practiced violin.
But she came out for piano.
At night she played sonatas
on my quilt.
One cat built a secret nest
in my socks.
One sat in the window
staring up at the street all day
while we were at school.
One cat loved the radio dial.
One cat almost smiled.

POEM

As the cat
climbed over
the top of

the jamcloset
first the right
forefoot

carefully
then the hind
stepped down

into the pit of
the empty
flower pot

THE CHESHIRE CAT
From *Alice's Adventures in Wonderland*

'I said "pig",' replied Alice; 'and I wish you wouldn't keep appearing and vanishing so suddenly: you make one quite giddy!'

'All right,' said the Cat; and this time it vanished quite slowly, beginning with the end of the tail, and ending with the grin, which remained some time after the rest of it had gone.

'Well! I've often seen a cat without a grin,' thought Alice; 'but a grin without a cat! It's the most curious thing I ever saw in all my life!'

THIS IS MY CHAIR

This is my chair.
Go away and sit somewhere else.
This one is all my own.
It is the only thing in your house that I possess
And insist upon possessing.
Everything else therein is yours.
My dish,
My toys,
My basket,
My scratching post and my Ping-Pong ball;
You provided them for me.
This chair I selected for myself.
I like it,
It suits me.
You have the sofa,
The stuffed chair
And the footstool.
I don't go and sit on them do I?
Then why cannot you leave me mine,
And let us have no further argument?

THE CAT AND THE WIND

A small wind
blows across the hedge
into the yard.
The cat cocks her ears
 – multitudinous rustling
and crackling all around –
her pupils dwindle
to specks in
her yellow eyes
that stare first upward
and then on every side
unable to single out
any one thing
to pounce on,
for all together
as if orchestrated,
twigs, leaves,
small pebbles, pause
and start and pause
in their shifting,
their rubbing
against each other.

She is still listening
when the wind is already
three gardens off.

THOM GUNN   89

CAT

Again and again through the day
I meet a cat.
In the tree's shade, in the sun, in the crowding
    brown leaves.
After the success of a few fish bones
Or inside a skeleton of white earth
I find it, as absorbed in the purring
Of its heart as a bee.
Still it sharpens its claws on the gulmohar tree
And follows the sun all day long.

Now I see it and then it is gone,
Losing itself somewhere.
On the autumn evening I have watched it play,
Stroking the soft body of the saffron sun
With a white paw. Then it caught
The darkness in paws like small balls
And scattered it all over the earth.

From THE CAT IN THE HAT

'Look at me!
Look at me now!' said the cat.
'With a cup and a cake
On the top of my hat!
I can hold up TWO books!
I can hold up the fish!
And a little toy ship!
And some milk on a dish!
And look!
I can hop up and down on the ball!
But that is not all!
Oh, no.
That is not all ...'

THEODOR SEUSS GEISEL (DR SEUSS)   91

CAT JACKS

Do not play jacks
With the Jaguar cat –
You'll never ever beat her.
If she don't win,
She'll start to whine.
If she gets an eight,
She'll pick up nine –
She'll say she didn't,
But you'll know she's lion –
She's such an awful Cheetah.

THE CATS OF KILKENNY

There once were two cats of Kilkenny,
Each thought there was one cat too many.
So they fought and they fit,
And they scratched and they bit,
Till, excepting their nails
And the tips of their tails,
Instead of two cats, there weren't any.

ANON.

NINE FAT CATS IN LITTLE ITALY

Say buon giorn to fatso Toni
   She likes to gorge on peperoni.
Ignazio gatto feels so lucky
   When he's stuffed with molti gnocchi.
Our favorite kitty Carolina
   Mangia bene on pastina.
Caruso cat sings for salami
   With parmesan and vermicelli.
The bandit tomcat Lee Gumba'ro
   Steals the sausage of San Gennaro.
Padrone cat Marloni Brando
   Prays last rites for cannellono.
The royal feline Medici
   Drinks champagne with biscotti.
When it comes to frutt' di mari
   A cat called Est chews calamari.
Laura loves her antipasta
   Prosciutto, pesce and polenta,
   Risotto, ragu, rigatoni
   And Yankee Doodle macaroni!

DEAR COMPANION

'There are two means of refuge from the miseries
of life: music and cats.'

ALBERT SCHWEITZER

PANGUR BÁN

*(Written in Gaelic by a student of the
monastery of Corinthia on a copy of
St Paul's Epistles, in the eighth century.)*

I and Pangur Bán, my cat,
'Tis a like task we are at:
Hunting mice is his delight,
Hunting words I sit all night.

Better far than praise of men
'Tis to sit with book and pen;
Pangur bears me no ill-will,
He too plies his simple skill.

'Tis a merry thing to see
At our tasks how glad are we,
When at home we sit and find
Entertainment to our mind.

Oftentimes a mouse will stray
In the hero Pangur's way;
Oftentimes my keen thought set
Takes a meaning in its net.

'Gainst the wall he sets his eye
Full and fierce and sharp and sly;

'Gainst the wall of knowledge I
All my little wisdom try.

When a mouse darts from its den,
O how glad is Pangur then!
O what gladness do I prove
When I solve the doubts I love!

So in peace our tasks we ply,
Pangur Bán, my cat, and I;
In our arts we find our bliss,
I have mine and he has his.

Practice every day has made
Pangur perfect in his trade;
I get wisdom day and night
Turning darkness into light.

     TR. ROBIN FLOWER

MORNING

Salt shining behind its glass cylinder.
Milk in a blue bowl. The yellow linoleum.
The cat stretching her black body from the pillow.
The way she makes her curvaceous response to the
    small, kind gesture.
Then laps the bowl clean.
Then wants to go out into the world
where she leaps lightly and for no apparent reason
    across the lawn,
then sits, perfectly still, in the grass.
I watch her a little while, thinking:
what more could I do with wild words?
I stand in the cold kitchen, bowing down to her.
I stand in the cold kitchen, everything wonderful
    around me.

APARTMENT CATS

The Girls wake, stretch, and pad up to the door.
    They rub my leg and purr;
    One sniffs around my shoe,
    Rich with an outside smell,
  The other rolls back on the floor –
White bib exposed, and stomach of soft fur.

Now, more awake, they re-enact Ben Hur
    Along the corridor,
    Wheel, gallop; as they do,
    Their noses twitching still,
  Their eyes get wild, their bodies tense,
Their usual prudence seemingly withdraws.

And then they wrestle: parry, lock of paws,
    Blind hug of close defense,
    Tail-thump, and smothered mew.
    If either, though, feels claws,
  She abruptly rises, knowing well
How to stalk off in wise indifference.

From TO A CAT

Stately, kindly, lordly friend,
   Condescend
Here to sit by me, and turn
Glorious eyes that smile and burn,
Golden eyes, love's lustrous meed,
On the golden page I read.

All your wondrous wealth of hair,
   Dark and fair,
Silken-shaggy, soft and bright
As the clouds and beams of night,
Pays my reverent hand's caress
Back with friendlier gentleness.

Dogs may fawn on all and some
   As they come;
You, a friend of loftier mind,
Answer friends alone in kind.
Just your foot upon my hand
Softly bids it understand.

ALGERNON CHARLES SWINBURNE   101

From THE SPINSTER'S SWEET-ARTS

I

Milk for my sweet-arts, Bess! fur it mun be the time
   about now
When Molly cooms in fro' the far-end close wi' her
   paäils fro' the cow.
Eh! tha be new to the plaäce – thou 'rt gaäpin' –
   does n't tha see
I calls 'em arter the fellers es once was sweet upo' me?

II

Naäy, to be sewer, it be past 'er time.
What maäkes 'er sa laäte?
Goä to the laäne at the back, an' looök thruf
   Maddison's gaäte!

III

Sweet-arts! Molly belike may 'a lighted to-night
   upo' one.
Sweet-arts! thanks to the Lord that I niver not listen'd
   to noän!
So I sits i' my oän armchair wi' my oän kettle theere
   o' the hob,
An' Tommy the fust, an' Tommy the second, an'
   Steevie an' Rob.

IV

Rob, coom oop 'ere o' my knee. Thou sees that i' spite
    o' the men
I 'a kep' thruf thick an' thin my two 'oonderd a-year
    to mysen;
Yis! thaw tha call'd me es pretty es ony lass i' the Shere;
An' thou be es pretty a tabby, but Robby I seed thruf
    ya theere.

V

Feyther 'ud saäy I wur ugly es sin, an' I beänt not vaäin,
But I niver wur downright hugly, thaw soom 'ud 'a
    thowt ma plaäin,
An' I was n't sa plaäin i' pink ribbons – ye said I wur
    pretty i' pinks,
An' I liked to 'ear it I did, but I beänt sich a fool as
    ye thinks;
Ye was stroäkin' ma down wi' the 'air, as I be a-stroäkin'
    o' you,
But whiniver I looöked i' the glass I wur sewer that it
    could n't be true;
Niver wur pretty, not I, but ye knaw'd it wur pleasant
    to 'ear,
Thaw it warn't not me es wur pretty, but my two
    'oonderd a-year.

ALFRED, LORD TENNYSON

From DAME WIGGINS OF
LEE AND HER SEVEN
WONDERFUL CATS

Dame Wiggins of Lee
    Was a worthy old soul
As e'er threaded a nee-
    dle or wash'd in a bowl:

She held mice and rats
    In such antipathee,
That seven fine cats
    Kept Dame Wiggins of Lee.

The rats and mice scared
    By this fierce-whiskered crew,
The poor seven cats
    Soon had nothing to do;

So, as anyone idle
    She ne'er loved to see,
She sent them to school,
    Did Dame Wiggins of Lee.

The master soon wrote
      That they all of them knew
How to read the word 'milk'
      And to spell the word 'mew,'

And they all washed their faces
      Before they took tea.
Were there ever such dears?
      Said Dame Wiggins of Lee.

From TWO SONGS OF A FOOL

A speckled cat and a tame hare
Eat at my hearthstone
And sleep there;
And both look up to me alone
For learning and defence
As I look up to Providence.

I start out of my sleep to think
Some day I may forget
Their food and drink;
Or, the house door left unshut,
The hare may run till it's found
The horn's sweet note and the tooth of the hound.

I bear a burden that might well try
Men that do all by rule,
And what can I
That am a wandering-witted fool
But pray to God that He ease
My great responsibilities.

THE FLYING PETUNIAS

When I let the cat in I didn't see
that it had a mouse in its mouth. But then
it set the mouse down on the kitchen floor
and they proceeded to play cat and mouse.
How very apt, I thought. The mouse stood about
one foot from the cat and the cat would extend
one leg slowly and touch the mouse on its head.
The mouse would sort of bow in supplication.
Then the mouse would dash on and snuggle up
under the cat's belly. One time the mouse
ran up the cat's back and sat on the crook
of her neck, and the cat seemed calmly proud
to have it there. They kept me entertained
like this for about an hour, but then it
started to irritate me that they had this
all worked out so well and I threw the cat
out. The mouse ran under the kitchen sink.
I let kitty in when it was our bedtime.
She has her pillow and I have mine and we've
always slept very sweetly together. In the
middle of this night, however, I feel these
tiny feet creeping across my neck and onto
my chin. I open my eyes slowly and kitty
is staring at me from her pillow and I am
staring at her. Then I close my eyes and
she closes hers and we all three dream of
joining the circus.

JAMES TATE   107

WHO WILL FEED MY CAT?

I

Will need

Someone to feed my cat

When I leave this world,

Though my cat is not ordinary.

She only has three paws:

Fire, air,

Water.

CAT IN AN EMPTY APARTMENT

Die – you can't do that to a cat.
Since what can a cat do
in an empty apartment?
Climb the walls?
Rub up against the furniture?
Nothing seems different here,
but nothing is the same.
Nothing has been moved,
but there's more space.
And at nighttime no lamps are lit.

Footsteps on the staircase,
but they're new ones.
The hand that puts fish on the saucer
has changed, too.

Something doesn't start
at its usual time.
Something doesn't happen
as it should.
Someone was always, always here,
then suddenly disappeared
and stubbornly stays disappeared.

Every closet has been examined.
Every shelf has been explored.
Excavations under the carpet turned up nothing.
A commandment was even broken:
papers scattered everywhere.
What remains to be done.
Just sleep and wait.

Just wait till he turns up,
just let him show his face.
Will he ever get a lesson
on what not to do to a cat.
Sidle toward him
as if unwilling
and ever so slow
on visibly offended paws,
and no leaps or squeals at least to start.

From THE CAT AND THE COCK

Once a certain cat and cock,
Friendship founded on a rock,
Lived together in a house
In the land of Fledermaus.
Each loved music in his way,
And the cock, at break of day
Chanted: 'Cock-a-doodle-doo!
Kiki-riki – Kuk-ru-koo!',
While his cat-friend, in the middle
Of the night, would play the fiddle.
Sometimes they would play together
– Handsome fur and fancy feather –
And the pair would dance and sing
While the house with joy would ring.

THE CATS HAVE COME TO TEA

What did she see – oh, what did she see,
As she stood leaning against the tree?
Why all the Cats had come to tea.

What a fine turn out – from round about,
All the houses had let them out,
And here they were with scamper and shout.

'Mew – mew – mew!' was all they could say,
And, 'We hope we find you well to-day.'

Oh, what should she do – oh, what should she do?
What a lot of milk they would get through;
For here they were with 'Mew – mew – mew!'

She didn't know – oh, she didn't know,
If bread and butter they'd like or no;
They might want little mice, oh! oh! oh!

Dear me – oh, dear me,
All the cats had come to tea.

THE AMOROUS CAT

'When I play with my cat, who knows if she is not amusing herself with me more than I with her.'

MICHEL DE MONTAIGNE

THE CAT

Come here, kitty – sheathe your claws!
   Lie on my loving heart
and let me sink into your eyes
   of agate fused with steel.

When my fingers freely caress
   your head and supple spine,
and my hand thrills to the touch
   of your electric fur,

my mistress comes to mind. Her gaze –
   cold and deep as yours,
my pet – is like a stab of pain,

   and from head to heels
a subtle scent, a dangerous perfume,
   rises from her brown flesh.

THE LOVER, WHOSE MISTRESSE FEARED A MOUSE, DECLARETH THAT HE WOULD BECOME A CAT IF HE MIGHT HAVE HIS DESIRE

If I might alter kind,
    What, think you, I would be?
Not Fish, nor Foule, nor Fle, nor Frog,
    Nor Squirrel on the Tree;
The Fish, the Hooke, the Foule
    The lymèd Twig doth catch,
The Fle, the Finger, and the Frog
    The Bustard doth dispatch.

The Squirrel thinking nought,
    That feately cracks the nut;
The greedie Goshawke wanting prey,
    In dread of Death doth put;
But scorning all these kindes,
    I would become a Cat,
To combat with the creeping Mouse,
    And scratch the screeking Rat.

I would be present, aye,
    And at my Ladie's call,
To gard her from the fearfull Mouse,
    In Parlour and in Hall;

In Kitchen, for his Lyfe,
    He should not shew his hed;
The Pease in Poke should lie untoucht
    When shee were gone to Bed.

The Mouse should stand in Feare,
    So should the squeaking Rat;
All this would I doe if I were
    Converted to a Cat.

MY CAT AND I

Girls are simply the prettiest things
My cat and i believe
And we're always saddened
When it's time for them to leave

We watch them titivating
(that often takes a while)
And though they keep us waiting
My cat and i just smile

We like to see them to the door
Say how sad it couldn't last
Then my cat and i go back inside
And talk about the past.

PROPRIETY

Cats making love in the temple
But people would blame
A man and wife for mating in such a place.

KAWAI CHIGETSU-NI
TR. KENNETH REXROTH AND IKUKO ATSUMI

PUSSYCAT SITS ON A CHAIR

Pussycat sits on a chair
Implacably with acid stare.

Those who early loved in vain
Use the cat to try again,

And test their bruised omnipotence
Against the cat's austere defense.

EDWARD NEWMAN HORN

AN APPEAL TO CATS IN THE BUSINESS OF LOVE

Ye cats that at midnight spit love at each other,
Who best feel the pangs of a passionate lover,
I appeal to your scratches and your tattered fur,
If the business of love be no more than to purr.
Old Lady Grimalkin with her gooseberry eyes,
Knew something when a kitten, for why she is wise;
You find by experience, the love-fit's soon o'er,
Puss! Puss! lasts not long, but turns to *Cat-whore!*
      Men ride many miles,
      Cats tread many tiles,
   Both hazard their necks in the fray;
      Only cats, when they fall
      From a house or a wall,
  Keep their feet, mount their tails, and away!

Arise from sleep, old cat,
And with great yawns and stretchings
Amble out for love.

ISSA

Why so scrawny, cat?
Starving for fat fish or mice ...
Or backyard love?

BASHŌ

Amorous cat, alas
You too must yowl with your love ...
Or even worse, without!

YAHA

THE CATS OF BALTHUS

We must bear witness to something.
At the Château de Chassy, near Autun,
Balthus Klossowski de Rola eats breakfast
under the green eye of Mitsou, Angora.

In the painter's eye girls forever
sprawl like morning sun among the hassocks
and fainting-sofas. They drink tea
the color of sunrise and as bitter.

At the Château de Chassy the sun
tries hard to be nameless in spite
of the painter's eye and will
to tame it, drape it across the proper chair.

But he will not tame the cats,
and only pretends to name them
for the neighbors' sake. They drape
where they like, leave their marks

on the muslin, chew through the doilies
the shape of white suns; they leave
their film of hair thickening
on the furniture. They sprawl.

We would like to look at the girls
doomed to adolescence, to see them
through the wide windows he offers us
as if we, on the way home late,

the evening's carouse given way
to gray sunrise, were caught by the slight
movement of girls in the house; as if
we stand in the shrubbery to look

then notice ourselves noticed
by the cat, its green eye narrowing
as if we both stare at the jungled coast
of wilderness and wanton desire.

CATS

A cat is not a person, you say,
not a Christian –
I have seen many!
Playing with mice who sat on their tails
    squeaking out protest
Then let them go
to die by themselves of shock
without wounds other than small claw-marks
little love-bites.

ALLEY CAT LOVE SONG

Come into the garden, Fred,
For the neighborhood tabby is gone.
Come into the garden, Fred.
I have nothing but my flea collar on,
And the scent of catnip has gone to my head.
I'll wait by the screen door till dawn.

The fireflies court in the sweetgum tree.
The nightjar calls from the pine,
And she seems to say in her rhapsody,
'Oh, mustard-brown Fred, be mine!'
The full moon lights my whiskers afire,
And the fur goes erect on my spine.

I hear the frogs in the muddy lake
Croaking from shore to shore.
They've one swift season to soothe their ache.
In autumn they sing no more.
So ignore me now, and you'll hear my meow
As I scratch all night at the door.

DANA GIOIA   125

A LOST PAINTING BY BALTHUS

A large blond Siamese cat
with the grave face and stern eyes
of an old Don Juan, stretches full length
along the body of a red-haired girl
on a blue chaise longue, her arms thrown back.

They lie as close as the two sides,
fur and skin, of a smooth sable pelt,
two slices cut from the same apple, or
the tender, perfumed, overlapping disks
of 'Gloire de Dijon' rose petals.

WOMAN AND CAT

As she sported with Pussy,
hand and paw, identically white,
were marvelous to see
jousting in evening light.

Deadly chalcedony nails
bright and sharp as a blade
hid beneath black-stitched gloves
which the cunning one had made.

In sugared dissimulation
the cat hid sharpened claws,
devilishly bold.

Behind the boudoir screen
where its airy laughter tolled,
four points of phosphorus gleamed.

PAUL VERLAINE   127
TR. BENJAMIN IVRY

THE OWL AND THE PUSSY-CAT

The Owl and the Pussy-cat went to sea
   In a beautiful pea-green boat,
They took some honey, and plenty of money,
   Wrapped up in a five-pound note.
The Owl looked up to the stars above,
   And sang to a small guitar,
'O lovely Pussy! O Pussy, my love,
   What a beautiful Pussy you are,
     You are,
     You are!
   What a beautiful Pussy you are!'

Pussy said to the Owl, 'You elegant fowl!
   How charmingly sweet you sing!
O let us be married! too long we have tarried:
   But what shall we do for a ring?'
They sailed away, for a year and a day,
   To the land where the Bong-Tree grows,
And there in a wood a Piggy-wig stood,
   With a ring at the end of his nose,
     His nose,
     His nose,
   With a ring at the end of his nose.

'Dear Pig, are you willing to sell for one shilling
    Your ring?' Said the Piggy, 'I will.'
So they took it away, and were married next day
    By the Turkey who lives on the hill.
They dined on mince, and slices of quince,
    Which they ate with a runcible spoon;
And hand in hand, on the edge of the sand,
    They danced by the light of the moon,
        The moon,
        The moon,
    They danced by the light of the moon.

EDWARD LEAR

CURSE OF THE CAT WOMAN

It sometimes happens
that the woman you meet and fall in love with
is of that strange Transylvanian people
with an affinity for cats.

You take her to a restaurant, say, or a show,
on an ordinary date, being attracted
by the glitter in her slitty eyes and her catlike walk,
and afterwards of course you take her in your arms
and she turns into a black panther
and bites you to death.

Or perhaps you are saved in the nick of time
and she is tormented by the knowledge of her tendency:
That she daren't hug a man
unless she wants to risk clawing him up.

This puts you both in a difficult position –
panting lovers who are prevented from touching
not by bars but by circumstance:
You have terrible fights and say cruel things
for having the hots does not give you a sweet temper.

One night you are walking down a dark street
and hear the pad-pad of a panther following you,
but when you turn around there are only shadows,
or perhaps one shadow too many.

You approach, calling, 'Who's there?'
and it leaps on you.
Luckily you have brought along your sword
and you stab it to death.

And before your eyes it turns into the woman you love,
her breast impaled on your sword,
her mouth dribbling blood saying she loved you
but couldn't help her tendency.

So death released her from the curse at last,
and you knew from the angelic smile on her dead face
that in spite of a life the devil owned,
love had won, and heaven pardoned her.

SLEEPING,
DREAMING

'The cat pretends to sleep that it may see the
more clearly.'

CHATEAUBRIAND

LULLABY FOR THE CAT

Minnow, go to sleep and dream
    Close your great big eyes;
Round your bed Events prepare
    The pleasantest surprise.

Darling Minnow, drop that frown,
    Just cooperate,
Not a kitten shall be drowned
    In the Marxist State.

Joy and Love will both be yours,
    Minnow, don't be glum.
Happy days are coming soon –
    Sleep, and let them come.

THE HAPPY CAT

The cat's asleep; I whisper *kitten*
Till he stirs a little and begins to purr –
He doesn't wake. Today out on the limb
(The limb he thinks he can't climb down from)
He mewed until I heard him in the house.
I climbed up to get him down: he mewed.
What he says and what he sees are limited.
My own response is even more constricted.
I think, 'It's lucky; what you have is too.'
What do you have except – well, me?
I joke about it but it's not a joke:
The house and I are all he remembers.
Next month how will he guess that it is winter
And not just entropy, the universe
Plunging at last into its cold decline?
I cannot think of him without a pang.
Poor rumpled thing, why don't you see
That you have no more, really, than a man?
Men aren't happy: why are you?

CAT ON THE MAT

The fat cat on the mat
    may seem to dream
of nice mice that suffice
    for him, or cream;
but he is free, maybe,
    walks in thought
unbowed, proud, where loud
    roared and fought
his kin, lean and slim,
    or deep in den
in the East feasted on beasts
    and tender men.

The giant lion with iron
    claw in paw,
and huge ruthless tooth
    in gory jaw;
the pard dark-starred
    fleet upon feet,
that oft soft from aloft
    leaps on his meet
where words loom in gloom –
    far now they be
    fierce and free
    and tamed is he;
but fat cat on the mat
kept as pet
he does not forget.

J. R. R. TOLKIEN

CAT'S DREAM

How neatly a cat sleeps,
sleeps with its paws and its posture,
sleeps with its wicked claws,
and with its unfeeling blood,
sleeps with all the rings –
a series of burnt circles –
which have formed the odd geology
of its sand-colored tail.

I should sleep like a cat,
with all the fur of time,
with a tongue rough as flint,
with the dry sex of fire;
and after speaking to no one,
stretch myself over the world,
over the roofs and landscapes,
with a passionate desire
to hunt the rats in my dreams.

I have seen how the cat asleep
would undulate, how the night
flowed through it like dark water;
and at times, it was going to fall
or possibly plunge into
the bare deserted snowdrifts.

Sometimes it grew so much in sleep
like a tiger's great-grandfather,
and would leap in the darkness over
rooftops, clouds and volcanoes.

Sleep, sleep, cat of the night
with episcopal ceremony
and your stone-carved moustache.
Take care of all our dreams;
control the obscurity
of our slumbering prowess
with your relentless heart
and the great ruff of your tail.

From PETER

   Strong and slippery,
built for the midnight grass-party
confronted by four cats he sleeps his time away –
the detached first claw on the foreleg corresponding
to the thumb, retracted to its tip; the small tuft of
      fronds
or katydid-legs above each eye numbering all units
in each group; the shadbones regularly set about the
      mouth
to droop or rise in unison like porcupine-quills.
He lets himself be flattened out by gravity,
as seaweed is tamed and weakened by the sun,
compelled when extended, to lie stationary.
Sleep is the result of his delusion that one must
do as well as one can for oneself,
sleep – epitome of what is to him the end of life.
Demonstrate on him how the lady placed a forked stick
on the innocuous neck-sides of the dangerous southern
      snake.
One need not try to stir him up; his prune-shaped head
and alligator-eyes are not party to the joke.
Lifted and handled, he may be dangled like an eel
or set up on the forearm like a mouse;
his eyes bisected by pupils of a pin's width,
are flickeringly exhibited, then covered up.

CAT

By the fire, like drifting reddish goldfish,
the cat dozed, curled within itself.
If, by mischance, I were to stir,
the cat might change to something else.

The spinning-wheel of ancient magic
must never be allowed to stick:
and changing itself into a princess
is, for the cat, a minor trick.

JEAN COCTEAU
TR. ALASTAIR REID

CATS SLEEP FAT
(From *Catalogue*)

Cats sleep fat and walk thin.
Cats, when they sleep, slump;
When they wake, stretch and begin
Over, pulling their ribs in.
Cats walk thin.

Cats wait in a lump,
Jump in a streak.
Cats, when they jump, are sleek
As a grape slipping its skin –
They have technique.
Oh, cats don't creak.
They sneak.

Cats sleep fat.
They spread out comfort underneath them
Like a good mat,
As if they picked the place
And then sat;
You walk around one
As if he were the City Hall
After that.

CATSNEST

Tread.

Tread.

Our cat treads my bed,
Pushing my spread to a heap for his sleep,
Punching sheets, stretching his tailbone up tall –
That it's me underneath doesn't matter at all –

And at last when he's hollowed a hollow he likes
He fits down inside it and, satisfied, purrs
Until Grandmother comes in to turn out my light
And to tell me good night. Then he angrily stirs
And he fluffs up gigantic and glowers, to say:
Well, I did all that digging – why shouldn't I stay?

CAT & THE WEATHER

Cat takes a look at the weather.
Snow.
Puts a paw on the sill.
His perch is piled, is a pillow.

Shape of his pad appears.
Will it dig? No.
Not like sand.
Like his fur almost.

But licked, not liked.
Too cold.
Insects are flying, fainting down.
He'll try

to bat one against the pane.
They have no body and no buzz.
And now his feet are wet;
it's a puzzle.

Shakes each leg,
then shakes his skin
to get the white flies off.
Looks for his tail,

tells it to come on in
by the radiator.
World's turned queer
somehow. All white,

no smell. Well, here
inside it's still familiar.
He'll go to sleep until
it puts itself right.

ON THE PROWL

'The cat, with eyne of burning coal,
Now couches fore the mouse's hole.'

SHAKESPEARE

VERSES ON A CAT

A cat in distress,
 Nothing more, nor less;
Good folks, I must faithfully tell ye,
 As I am a sinner,
 It waits for some dinner,
To stuff out its own little belly.

You would not easily guess,
 All the modes of distress
Which torture the tenants of earth;
 And the various evils,
 Which, like so many devils,
Attend the poor souls from their birth.

Some living require,
 And others desire
An old fellow out of the way;
 And which is best
 I leave to be guessed,
For I cannot pretend to say.

One wants society,
 Another variety,
Others a tranquil life;
 Some want food,
 Others, as good,
Only want a wife.

But this poor little cat
    Only wanted a rat,
To stuff out its own little maw;
    And it were as good
    Some people had such food,
To make them *hold their jaw!*

FIVE EYES

In Hans' old mill his three black cats
Watch his bins for thieving rats.
Whisker and claw, they crouch in the night,
Their five eyes smouldering green and bright:
Squeaks from the flour sacks, squeaks from where
The cold wind stirs on the empty stair,
Squeaking and scampering, everywhere.
Then down they pounce, now in, now out,
At whisking tail, and sniffing snout;
While lean old Hans he snores away
Till peep of light at break of day;
Then up he climbs to his creaking mill,
Out come his cats all grey with meal – Jekkel, and
      Jessup, and one-eyed Jill.

THE CAT

You get a wife, you get a house,
Eventually you get a mouse.
You get some words regarding mice,
You get a kitty in a trice.
By two A.M. or thereabout,
The mouse is in, the cat is out.
It dawns upon you, in your cot,
The mouse is silent, the cat is not.
Instead of Pussy, says your spouse,
You should have bought another mouse.

'PUSSY-CAT, PUSSY-CAT'

'Pussy-cat, Pussy-cat,
    Where have you been?'
'I've been to London,
    To look at the Queen.'
'Pussy-cat, Pussy-cat,
    What did you there?'
'I frightened a little mouse
    Under her chair.'

'THERE WAS A WEE
BIT MOUSIKIE'

There was a wee bit mousikie,
    That lived in Gilberaty, O;
It couldna get a bite o' cheese,
    For cheety-poussie-catty, O.

It said unto the cheesikie,
    'Oh, fain wad I be at ye, O,
If it were na for the cruel paws
    O' cheety-poussie-catty, O.'

ANON.   153

THE RAT-CATCHER AND CATS

The rats by night such mischief did,
Betty was ev'ry morning chid.
They undermined whole sides of bacon,
Her cheese was sapp'd, her tarts were taken.
Her pasties, fenced with thickest paste,
Were all demolish'd, and laid waste.
She cursed the Cat for want of duty,
Who left her foes a constant booty.

    An engineer, of noted skill,
Engaged to stop the growing ill.

    From room to room he now surveys
Their haunts, their works, their secret ways;
Finds where they 'scape an ambuscade,
And whence the nightly sally's made.

    An envious Cat from place to place,
Unseen, attends his silent pace.
She saw that if his trade went on,
The purring race must be undone;
So, secretly removes his baits,
And ev'ry stratagem defeats.

    Again he sets the poison'd toils,
And Puss again the labour foils.

    What foe (to frustrate my designs)
My schemes thus nightly countermines?
Incensed, he cries, this very hour
The wretch shall bleed beneath my power.

So said, a pond'rous trap he brought,
And in the fact poor Puss was caught.

Smuggler, says he, thou shalt be made
A victim to our loss of trade.

The captive Cat, with piteous mews,
For pardon, life, and freedom sues.
A sister of the science spare;
One int'rest is our common care.

What insolence! the man replied;
Shall Cats with us the game divide?
Were all your interloping band
Extinguish'd, or expell'd the land,
We Rat-catchers might raise our fees,
Sole guardians of a nation's cheese!

A Cat, who saw the lifted knife,
Thus spoke, and saved her sister's life:

In ev'ry age and clime we see,
Two of a trade can ne'er agree.
Each hates his neighbour for encroaching;
'Squire stigmatizes 'squire for poaching;
Beauties with beauties are in arms,
And scandal pelts each other's charms;
Kings, too, their neighbour kings dethrone,
In hope to make the world their own.
But let us limit our desires,
Not war like beauties, kings, and 'squires!
For though we both one prey pursue,
There's game enough for us and you.

BY THREES, BY FOURS

Curly mousetail, mousetail, curly,
here's the housecat, hunting early.

Now's the time, and it's your time now,
time for chatting with my rhyme now.

Here's a mouth and here's its quelling,
here are words, hear them rebelling.

Open spaces, narrow scrapings,
near catastrophes we're facing.

You and me too, then we threesome,
half in fetters, half in freedom.

Curly mousetail, mousetail, curly,
here's the housecat, hunting early.

156 PAUL CELAN
    TR. JOHN FELSTINER

From THE MAUNCIPLE'S TALE

Lat take a cat a fostre hym wel with milk
And tendre flessh, and make his couche of silk,
And lay him seen a mous go by the wal,
Anon he weyveth milk and flessh and al
And every deyntee that is in that hous
Swich appetit hath he to ete a mous.

GEOFFREY CHAUCER

CAT AND MOUSE

On the sheep-cropped summit, under hot sun,
The mouse crouched, staring out the chance
It dared not take.
       Time and a world
Too old to alter, the five mile prospect –
Woods, villages, farms – hummed its heat-heavy
Stupor of life.
                   Whether to two
Feet or four, how are prayers contracted!
Whether in God's eye or the eye of a cat.

TED HUGHES   157

'MY HERMITAGE'

My hermitage is home to a cat and a mouse;
Both are furry creatures.
The cat is fat and sleeps in broad daylight;
The mouse is thin and scampers about in the dark.
The cat is blessed with talent,
Able to deftly catch living things for its meals.
The mouse is cursed,
Limited to sneaking bits and pieces of food.
A mouse can damage containers, it is true,
But containers can be replaced,
Not so living things.
If you ask me which creature incurs more sin,
I'd say the cat!

TR. JOHN STEVENS

THE OLD CAT AND THE YOUNG MOUSE

Miss Mouse, young both in years and experience,
Addressed old Champ Cat with tears and soft eloquence
Hoping to move him to mercy, though she was caught.
    'Let me live, do. I'm small. I'm short.
    I survive at no one's expense.
    Surely your household can afford
    The grain a day that is my board.
    A whole walnut once made me sick!
    Truly. It made me look, my lord,
    Like a pumpkin tied to a stick.
Time will augment my stature. Commute my sentence,
And I'll make a tasty feast for your descendants.'
The old cat cleared his throat and addressed his captive.
    'Cats my age are not adaptive.
You young ones think talk can change the fate of nations.
A deafening gulf roars between generations.
An old cat, merciful? I've never heard of it.
    Die, and tell the Fates your sad tale.
   As for me, I must say I fail
   To understand a word of it.
As for my sons, they can fill their own dinner pail.'
    He ate the mouse. To my mind
This shows both silly, self-satisfied youth basking
In the thought that the world is theirs for the asking,
    And hateful age, hard and unkind.

JEAN DE LA FONTAINE   159
TR. MARIE PONSOT

CAT

He is all black, but has an electric tail. When he sleeps in the sun he is the blackest thing one can imagine. Even in his sleep he catches frightened mice. One can see this in the little claws that are growing from his paws. He is terribly nice and naughty. He picks birds off the trees before they are ripe.

FOREST

A path runs barefoot to the forest. Inside are many trees, a cuckoo, Hansel and Gretel, and other small animals. But there are no dwarfs, because they have left. When it gets dark an owl closes the forest with a big key, for if a cat sneaked in it would really do a lot of harm.

THE LAZY PUSSY

There lives a good-for-nothing cat,
   So lazy it appears,
That chirping birds can safely come
   And light upon her ears.

And rats and mice can venture out
   To nibble at her toes,
Or climb around and pull her tail,
   And boldly scratch her nose.

Fine servants brush her silken coat
   And give her cream for tea; –
Yet she's a good-for-nothing cat,
   As all the world may see.

PALMER COX

'SHE SIGHTS A BIRD'

She sights a Bird – she chuckles –
She flattens – then she crawls –
She runs without the look of feet –
Her eyes increase to Balls –

Her Jaws stir – twitching – hungry –
Her Teeth can hardly stand –
She leaps, but Robin leaped the first –
Ah, Pussy, of the Sand,

The Hopes so juicy ripening –
You almost bathed your Tongue –
When Bliss disclosed a hundred Toes –
And fled with every one –

A CAT

She had a name among the children;
But no one loved though someone owned
Her, locked her out of doors at bedtime
And had her kittens duly drowned.

In Spring, nevertheless, this cat
Ate blackbirds, thrushes, nightingales,
And birds of bright voice and plume and flight,
As well as scraps from neighbours' pails.

I loathed and hated her for this;
One speckle on a thrush's breast
Was worth a million such; and yet
She lived long, till God gave her rest.

SONG OF THE LIONESS FOR HER CUB

Fear the one
who has sharp weapons
who wears a tassel of leopard tail,
he who has white dogs –
O son of the short-haired lioness!
My short-eared child,
son of the lioness who devours raw flesh,
you flesh-eater!
Son of the lioness whose nostrils are red with
     the bleeding prey,
you with the bloodred nostrils!
Son of the lioness who drinks water from the swamp,
You water-drinker!

CAT VS. DOG

'If animals could speak, the dog would be a
blundering, outspoken fellow, but the cat would have
the rare grace of never saying a word too much.'

MARK TWAIN

CATNIP AND DOGWOOD

A cat's quite different from a dog
And you name it differently, too;
A library cat might be Catalogue,
And a Siamese, Fu Manchu.
Dogs usually have humdrum names
Like Molly, Blacky, Biff, and James.

Cats eat catnip excitedly,
Get drunk and jump around,
But a dog can sniff at a dogwood tree,
And sniff and sniff quite diligently,
Sit down and never budge –
And be as smug and sober as a judge.

HOWARD MOSS

THE PRAYER OF THE CAT

Lord,
I am the cat.
It is not, exactly, that I have something to ask of You!
No –
I ask nothing of anyone –
but,
if You have by some chance, in some celestial barn,
a little white mouse,
or a saucer of milk,
I know someone who would relish them.
Wouldn't You like someday
to put a curse on the whole race of dogs?
If so I should say,

Amen

THE SINGLE CREATURE

DOG   The single creature leads a partial life,
        Man by his mind, and by his nose the hound;
        He needs the deep emotions I can give,
        I scent in him a vaster hunting ground.

CATS   Like calls to like, to share is to relieve,
        And sympathy the root bears love the flower;
        He feels in us, and we in him perceive
        A common passion for the lonely hour.

CATS   We move in our apartness and our pride,
        About the decent dwellings he has made:
DOG   In all his walks I follow at his side,
        His faithful servant and his loving shade.

W. H. AUDEN

A CAT'S CONSCIENCE

A dog will often steal a bone,
But conscience lets him not alone,
And by his tail his guilt is known.

But cats consider theft a game,
And, howsoever you may blame,
Refuse the slightest sign of shame.

When food mysteriously goes,
The chances are that Pussy knows
More than she leads you to suppose.

And hence there is no need for you,
If Puss declines a meal or two,
To feel her pulse and make ado.

MOTHER TABBYSKINS

Sitting at a window
In her cloak and hat,
I saw Mother Tabbyskins,
　　The *real* old cat!
　　　Very old, very old,
　　　　Crumplety and lame;
　　　Teaching kittens how to scold –
　　　　Is it not a shame?

Kittens in the garden
Looking in her face,
Learning how to spit and swear –
　　Oh, what a disgrace!
　　　Very wrong, very wrong,
　　　　Very wrong and bad;
　　　Such a subject for our song,
　　　　Makes us all too sad.

Old Mother Tabbyskins,
Sticking out her head,
Gave a howl, and then a yowl,
　　Hobbled off to bed.
　　　Very sick, very sick,
　　　　Very savage, too;
　　　Pray send for a doctor quick –
　　　　Any one will do!

Doctor Mouse came creeping,
  Creeping to her bed;
Lanced her gums and felt her pulse,
  Whispered she was dead.
    Very sly, very sly,
      The *real* old cat
Open kept her weather eye –
      Mouse! beware of that!

Old Mother Tabbyskins,
  Saying 'Serves him right',
Gobbled up the doctor, with
  Infinite delight.
    Very fast, very fast
    Very pleasant, too –
'What a pity it can't last!
    Bring another, do!'

Doctor Dog comes running,
  Just to see her begs;
Round his neck a comforter,
  Trousers on his legs.
    Very grand, very grand –
      Golden-headed cane
Swinging gaily from his hand,
      Mischief in his brain!

'Dear Mother Tabbyskins,
    And how are you now?
Let me feel your pulse – so, so;
    Show your tongue – bow, wow!
        Very ill, very ill,
        Please attempt to purr;
    Will you take a draught or pill?
        Which do you prefer?'

Ah, Mother Tabbyskins,
    Who is now afraid?
Of poor little Doctor Mouse
    You a mouthful made.
        Very nice, very nice
        Little doctor he;
    But for Doctor Dog's advice
        You must pay the fee.

Doctor Dog comes nearer,
    Says she must be bled;
I heard Mother Tabbyskins
    Screaming in her bed.
        Very near, very near,
        Scuffling out and in;
    Doctor Dog looks full and queer –
        Where is Tabbyskin?

I will tell the Moral
Without any fuss:
Those who lead the young astray
Always suffer thus.
Very nice, very nice,
Let our conduct be;
For all doctors are not mice,
Some are dogs, you see!

I MARRIED MY DOG

Last year, I married my dog.
Everyone came to see us
and we served dinner and dessert.

I was simply beautiful
and my dog looked nice, too.

My dog and I exchanged rings.
Then my dog gave me a flower
and I got very red.

That night, my dog and I went to bed.
We put on our nightgowns and fell asleep.

In the morning, I got up first.
I put on my clothes and went downstairs.
An hour later, my husband came down.
I said good morning
but he didn't notice.
He just lay on the floor, eating.

I was disappointed for a while.
But I soon fixed that!
I married my cat.

MARGARET KEMP ROSS   175

THE SCORNED CAT

'Do not laugh at a cat.'

INSTRUCTION OF ANKHSHESHONQ PTOLEMAIC PERIOD
(4TH–3RD CENTURIES B.C.)

'CONFOUND THE CATS!'

Confound the cats! All cats – alway –
    Cats of all colours, black, white, grey;
      By night a nuisance and by day –
        Confound the cats!

ORLANDO THOMAS DOBBIN

A FABLE OF THE WIDOW
AND HER CAT

A widow kept a favourite cat.
   At first a gentle creature;
But when he was grown sleek and fat,
With many a mouse, and many a rat,
   He soon disclosed his nature.

The fox and he were friends of old,
   Nor could they now be parted;
They nightly slunk to rob the fold,
Devoured the lambs, the fleeces sold,
   And puss grew lion-hearted.

He scratched her maid, he stole the cream,
   He tore her best laced pinner;
Nor Chanticleer upon the beam,
Nor chick, nor duckling 'scapes, when Grim
   Invites the fox to dinner.

The dame full wisely did decree,
   For fear he should dispatch more,
That the false wretch should worried be:
But in a saucy manner he
   Thus speeched it like a Lechmere.

'Must I, against all right and law,
    Like pole-cat vile be treated?
I! who so long with tooth and claw
Have kept domestic mice in awe,
    And foreign foes defeated!

'Your golden pippins, and your pies,
    How oft have I defended?
'Tis true, the pinner which you prize
I tore in frolic; to your eyes
    I never harm intended.

'I am a cat of honour – ' 'Stay,'
    Quoth she, 'no longer parley;
Whate'er you did in battle slay,
By law of arms become your prey,
    I hope you won it fairly.

'Of this, we'll grant you stand acquit,
    But not of your outrages:
Tell me, perfidious! was it fit
To make my cream a *perquisite*,
    And steal to mend your wages!

'So flagrant is thy insolence
  So vile thy breach of trust is;
That longer with thee to dispense,
Were want of power, or want of sense:
  Here, Towser! – Do him justice.'

THE CAT AND THE LUTE

Are these the strings that poets say
Have cleared the air, and calmed the sea?
Charmed wolves, and from the mountain crests
Made forests dance with all their beasts?
Could these neglected shreds you see
Inspire a lute of ivory
And make it speak? Oh! think then what
Hath been committed by my cat,
Who, in the silence of this night
Hath gnawed these cords, and ruined them quite,
Leaving such remnants as may be
'Frets' – not for my lute, but me.

Puss, I will curse thee; mayest thou dwell
With some dry hermit in a cell
Where rat ne'er peeped, where mouse ne'er fed,
And flies go supperless to bed.
Or may'st thou tumble from some tower,
And fail to land upon all fours,
Taking a fall that may untie
Eight of nine lives, and let them fly.

What, was there ne'er a rat nor mouse,
Nor larder open? nought in the house
But harmless lute-strings could suffice
Thy paunch, and draw thy glaring eyes?

Know then, thou wretch, that every string
Is a cat-gut, which men do spin
Into a singing thread: think on that,
Thou cannibal, thou monstrous cat!

Thou seest, puss, what evil might betide thee:
But I forbear to hurt or chide thee:

For maybe puss was melancholy
And so to make her blithe and jolly,
Finding these strings, she took a snatch
Of merry music: nay then, wretch,
Thus I revenge me, that as thou
Hast played on them, I've played on you.

From SAD MEMORIES

They tell me I am beautiful: they praise my silken hair,
My little feet that silently slip on from stair to stair:
They praise my pretty trustful face and innocent grey eye;
Fond hands caress me oftentimes, yet would that I
    might die!

Why was I born to be abhorred of man and bird and beast?
The bullfinch marks me stealing by, and straight his song
    hath ceased;
The shrewmouse eyes me shudderingly, then flees; and,
    worse than that,
The housedog he flees after me – why was I born a cat?

Men prize the heartless hound who quits dry-eyed his
    native land;
Who wags a mercenary tail and licks a tyrant hand.
The leal true cat they prize not, that if e'er compelled
    to roam
Still flies, when let out of the bag, precipitately home.

They call me cruel. Do I know if mouse or song-bird feels?
I only know they make me light and salutary meals:
And if, as 'tis my nature to, ere I devour I tease 'em,
Why should a low-bred gardener's boy pursue me with
    a besom?

CHARLES CALVERLY   185

JUSTICE

You expect, Puss-in-Boots
    to go on treating my house
as your house
    after treating my pet partridge
as a comestible?

No, pet partridge!
Over the bones of his treat
    the cat shall be slain,
and you honored in blood rite:
as Pyrrhus, recall,
(rightfully) slew
    Polyxena
over the corpse of Achilles.

TO MRS PROFESSOR
IN DEFENSE OF MY CAT'S HONOR
AND NOT ONLY

My valiant helper, a small-sized tiger
Sleeps sweetly on my desk, by the computer,
Unaware that you insult his tribe.

Cats play with a mouse or with a half-dead mole.
You are wrong, though: it's not out of cruelty.
They simply like a thing that moves.

For, after all, we know that only consciousness
Can for a moment move into the Other,
Empathize with the pain and panic of a mouse.

And such as cats are, all of Nature is.
Indifferent, alas, to the good and the evil.
Quite a problem for us, I am afraid.

Natural history has its museums,
But why should our children learn about monsters,
An earth of snakes and reptiles for millions of years?

Nature devouring, Nature devoured,
Butchery day and night smoking with blood.
And who created it? Was it the good Lord?

Yes, undoubtedly, they are innocent,
Spiders, mantises, sharks, pythons.
We are the only ones who say: cruelty.

Our consciousness and our conscience
Alone in the pale anthill of galaxies
Put their hope in a humane God.

Who cannot but feel and think,
Who is kindred to us by His warmth and movement,
For we are, as He told us, similar to Him.

Yet if it is so, then He takes pity
On every mauled mouse, every wounded bird.
Then the universe for Him is like a Crucifixion.

Such is the outcome of your attack on the cat:
A theological, Augustinian grimace,
Which makes difficult our walking on this earth.

TR. THE AUTHOR AND ROBERT HASS

From THE CHURLYSHE CAT

That vengeaunce I aske and crye,
By way of exclamacyon,
Of all the whole nacyon
Of cattes wylde and tame;
God send them sorowe and shame!
That cat especyally
That slew so cruelly
My lytell pretty sparowe,
That I brought up at Carowe.
    O cat of churlyshe kynde,
The Fynde was in thy minde
When thou my byrde untwynde!
I would thou haddest ben blynde!

JOHN SKELTON   189

EPITAPH

His friends he loved. His direst earthly foes –
  cats – I believe he did but feign to hate.
    My hand will miss the insinuated nose,
      Mine eyes the tail that wagged contempt at Fate.

KITTENS, KITTENS

'No matter how much cats fight, there always seem to be plenty of kittens.'

ABRAHAM LINCOLN

From THE KITTEN AND FALLING LEAVES

See the Kitten on the wall,
Sporting with the leaves that fall,
Withered leaves – one – two – and three –
From the lofty elder-tree!
Through the calm and frosty air
Of this morning bright and fair,
Eddying round and round they sink
Softly, slowly: one might think,
From the motions that are made,
Every little leaf conveyed
Sylph or Faery hither tending, –
To this lower world descending,
Each invisible and mute,
In his wavering parachute.
 – But the Kitten, how she starts,
Crouches, stretches, paws, and darts!
First at one, and then its fellow
Just as light and just as yellow;
There are many now – now one –
Now they stop and there are none:
What intenseness of desire
In her upward eye of fire!
With a tiger-leap half-way
Now she meets the coming prey,
Lets it go as fast, and then

Has it in her power again:
Now she works with three or four,
Like an Indian conjurer;
Quick as he in feats of art,
Far beyond in joy of heart.

CHAPLINESQUE

We make our meek adjustments,
Contented with such random consolations
As the wind deposits
In slithered and too ample pockets.

For we can still love the world, who find
A famished kitten on the step, and know
Recesses for it from the fury of the street,
Or warm torn elbow coverts.

We will sidestep, and to the final smirk
Dally the doom of that inevitable thumb
That slowly chafes its puckered index toward us,
Facing the dull squint with what innocence
And what surprise!

And yet these fine collapses are not lies
More than the pirouettes of any pliant cane;
Our obsequies are, in a way, no enterprise.
We can evade you, and all else but the heart:
What blame to us if the heart live on.

The game enforces smirks; but we have seen
The moon in lonely alleys make
A grail of laughter of an empty ash can,
And through all sound of gaiety and quest
Have heard a kitten in the wilderness.

HART CRANE   195

THE YOUNG CAT AND THE CHRYSANTHEMUMS

You mince, you start
advancing indirectly –
your tail upright
knocking about among the
frail heavily flowered
sprays.

Yes, you are lovely
with your ingratiating
manners, sleek sides and
small white paws, but
I wish you had not come
here.

BEWARE OF KITTENS

Beware, my friend, of fiends and their grimaces;
   Of little angels' wiles yet more beware thee;
   Just such a one to kiss her did ensnare me,
But coming, I got wounds and not embraces.
Beware of black old cats, with evil faces;
   Yet more, of kittens white and soft be wary;
   My sweetheart was just such a little fairy,
And yet she well-nigh scratched my heart to pieces.
Oh child! oh sweet love, dear beyond all measure,
   How could those eyes, so bright and clear,
     deceive me?
   That little paw so sore a heart-wound give me? –
My kitten's tender paw, thou soft, small treasure –
   Oh! could I to my burning lips but press thee,
   My heart the while might bleed to death and
     bless thee.

FAMILIARITY DANGEROUS

As in her ancient mistress' lap,
 The youthful tabby lay,
They gave each other many a tap,
 Alike dispos'd to play.

But strife ensues. Puss waxes warm,
 And with protruded claws
Ploughs all the length of Lydia's arm,
 Mere wantonness the cause.

At once, resentful of the deed,
 She shakes her to the ground
With many a threat, that she shall bleed
 With still a deeper wound.

But, Lydia, bid thy fury rest!
 It was a venial stroke;
For she, that will with kittens jest,
 Should bear a kitten's joke.

From THROUGH THE LOOKING-GLASS

It is a very inconvenient habit of kittens (Alice had once made the remark) that, whatever you say to them, they *always* purr. 'If they would only purr for "yes", and mew for "no", or any rule of that sort,' she had said, 'so that one could keep up a conversation! But how *can* you talk with a person if they always say the same thing?'

LEWIS CARROLL

DAWN

The little kitten's face
Like the sudden dawn
Swallows all of midnight
With a big pink yawn.

ANON.   199

PINKLE PURR

Tattoo was the mother of Pinkle Purr,
A little black nothing of feet and fur;
And by and by, when his eyes came through,
He saw his mother, the big Tattoo.
And all that he learned he learned from her,
'I'll ask my mother,' says Pinkle Purr.

Tattoo was the mother of Pinkle Purr,
A ridiculous kitten with silky fur.
And little black Pinkle grew and grew
Till he got as big as the big Tattoo.
And all he did he did with her.
'Two friends together,' says Pinkle Purr.

Tattoo was the mother of Pinkle Purr,
An adventurous cat in a coat of fur.
And whenever he thought of a thing to do,
He didn't much bother about Tattoo.
For he knows it's nothing to do with her,
So 'See you later,' says Pinkle Purr.

Tattoo was the mother of Pinkle Purr,
An enormous leopard with coal-black fur.
A little brown kitten that's nearly new
Is now playing games with its big Tattoo ...
And Pink looks lazily down at her:
'Dear little Tat,' says Pinkle Purr.

THE THREE LITTLE KITTENS

Three little kittens lost their mittens;
    And they began to cry,
        'Oh, mother dear,
        We very much fear
    That we have lost our mittens.'
        'Lost your mittens!
        You naughty kittens!
    Then you shall have no pie!'
        'Mee-ow, mee-ow, mee-ow.'
    'No, you shall have no pie.'
        'Mee-ow, mee-ow, mee-ow.'

The three little kittens found their mittens;
    And they began to cry,
        'Oh, mother dear,
        See here, see here!
    See, we have found our mittens!'
        'Put on your mittens,
        You silly kittens,
    And you may have some pie.'
        'Purr-r, purr-r, purr-r,
    Oh, let us have the pie!
        Purr-r, purr-r, purr-r.'

The three little kittens put on their mittens,
    And soon ate up the pie;
        'Oh, mother dear,
        We greatly fear
    That we have soiled our mittens!'
        'Soiled your mittens!
        You naughty kittens!'
    Then they began to sigh,
        'Mee-ow, mee-ow, mee-ow.'
    Then they began to sigh,
        'Mee-ow, mee-ow, mee-ow.'

The three little kittens washed their mittens,
    And hung them out to dry;
        'Oh, mother dear,
        Do not you hear
    That we have washed our mittens?'
        'Washed your mittens!
        Oh, you're good kittens!
    But I smell a rat close by,
        Hush, hush! Mee-ow, mee-ow.'
    'We smell a rat close by,
        Mee-ow, mee-ow, mee-ow.'

From THE KITTEN

Backward coil'd and crouching low,
With glaring eyeballs watch thy foe,
The housewife's spindle whirling round,
Or thread, or straw, that on the ground
Its shadow throws, by urchin sly
Held out to lure thy roving eye;
Then stealing onward, fiercely spring
Upon the tempting, faithless thing.
Now, whirling round with bootless skill,
Thy bo-peep tail provokes thee still,
As still beyond thy curving side
Its jetty tip is seen to glide;
Till from thy centre starting far,
Thou sidelong veer'st with rump in air
Erected stiff, and gait awry,
Like madam in her tantrums high;
Though ne-er a madam of them all,
Whose silken kirtle sweeps the hall,
More varied trick and whim displays
To catch the admiring stranger's gaze.

JOANNA BAILLIE   203

THE OLD CAT

'Cats and monkeys, monkeys and cats –
all human life is there.'

HENRY JAMES

TO A CAT

Cat! who hast pass'd thy grand climacteric,
　　How many mice and rats hast in thy days
　　Destroy'd? How many tit-bits stolen? Gaze
With those bright languid segments green, and prick
Those velvet ears – but prythee do not stick
　　Thy latent talons in me – and tell me all thy frays,
Of fish and mice, and rats and tender chick;
Nay, look not down, nor lick thy dainty wrists, –
　　For all the wheezy asthma – and for all
Thy tail's tip is nick'd off – and though the fists
　　Of many a maid have given thee many a maul,
Still is thy fur as when the lists
　　In youth thou enter'dst on glass-bottled wall.

ON A CAT, AGEING

He blinks upon the hearth-rug,
And yawns in deep content,
Accepting all the comforts
That Providence has sent.

Louder he purrs, and louder,
In one glad hymn of praise
For all the night's adventures,
For quiet restful days.

Life will go on forever,
With all that cat can wish,
Warmth and the glad procession
Of fish and milk and fish.

Only – the thought disturbs him –
He's noticed once or twice,
The times are somehow breeding
A nimbler race of mice.

HOPPY

Ancientest of cats, truest
model of decrepitude,
you shamble and push your own
sloppy shape across the room,
nosing the floor in your slow
unhappy step-by-step, and
with dollops of baby food
splashed around your whiskers, on
chin, on snout, and in one scarred
ear, don't you think it's gotten
crappy, this life, now the years
have slipped by, old Counselor?
You mop the rug with your tail,
you slap a tired paw against
the door, and turn dim yellow
eyes, flecked with a weariness
of having seen so much, back
over your jutting shoulder
to the faces that study
the exquisite mishap or
the dopey luck that has left
it to you – of all the world's
mopes and most unlikely wise,
prophets and poets – to stop
the bored chatter of these frail

merely human types and top
all their tiny, much boasted
perseverances with your
pained, apocalyptic glance.

A 14-YEAR-OLD CONVALESCENT CAT IN THE WINTER

I want him to have another living summer,
to lie in the sun and enjoy the *douceur de vivre* –
because the sun, like golden rum in a rummer,
is what makes an idle cat *un tout petit peu ivre* –

I want him to lie stretched out, contented,
revelling in the heat, his fur all dry and warm,
an Old Age Pensioner, retired, resented
by no one, and happinesses in a beelike swarm

to settle on him – postponed for another season
that last fated hateful journey to the vet
from which there is no return (and age the reason),
which must come soon – as I cannot forget.

MONTAGUE MICHAEL

Montague Michael
You're much too fat,
You wicked old, wily old,
Well-fed cat.

All night you sleep
On a cushion of silk,
And twice a day
I bring you milk.

And once in a while,
When you catch a mouse,
You're the proudest person
In all the house.

CAT

Old Mog comes in and sits on the newspaper
Old fat sociable cat
Thinks when we stroke him he's doing us a favour
Maybe he's right, at that.

JOAN AIKEN

DECEMBER CATS

Less and less they walk the wild
Cold world of dark, of windy snow.
Curiosity comes in;
There is nothing more to know;
Examines corners; yawns and dies,
Warm under lamps and buzzing flies.

The oldest beast, with panther head,
The latest yielded: ran in tracks
Himself had punctured; hid by stones
And pounced, and crackled mice's backs.
But now that all midwinter wests,
Even he the ranger rests.

MARK VAN DOREN

MY OLD CAT DANCES

He has conceived of a Republic of Mice
and a door through the fire,
parables of the reinstatement
of his balls. But not this night.
Isn't there a storm in the light bulb,
condors circling the kittens' meals
on the television screen?
He heard once that people wearied of
each other to escape unhappiness.
In his lovely sufficiency
he will string up endless garlands
for the moon's deaf guardians.
Moving one paw out and yawning,
he closes his eyes. Everywhere
people are in despair. And he is dancing.

ESTHER'S TOMCAT

Daylong this tomcat lies stretched flat
As an old rough mat, no mouth and no eyes,
Continual wars and wives are what
Have tattered his ears and battered his head.

Like a bundle of old rope and iron
Sleeps till blue dusk. Then reappear
His eyes, green as ringstones: he yawns wide red,
Fangs fine as a lady's needle and bright.

A tomcat sprang at a mounted knight,
Locked round his neck like a trap of hooks
While the knight rode fighting its clawing and bite.
After hundreds of years the stain's there

On the stone where he fell, dead of the tom:
That was at Barnborough. The tomcat still
Grallochs odd dogs on the quiet,
Will take the head clean off your simple pullet,

Is unkillable. From the dog's fury,
From gunshot fired point-blank he brings
His skin whole, and whole
From owlish moons of bekittenings

Among ashcans. He leaps and lightly
Walks upon sleep, his mind on the moon.
Nightly over the round world of men,
Over the roofs go his eyes and outcry.

From NINE LIVES

To all, sweet dreams. The teacup-stirring eddy
Is spent. We've dropped our masks, renewed our vows
To letters, to the lives that letters house,
Houses they shutter, streets they shade. Already
Empty and dark, this street is. Dusty boughs
Sleep in a pool of vigilance so bright
An old tom skirts it. The world's his tonight.

MOURNING
THE CAT

'A cat is an animal which has more human feelings
than almost any other.'

EMILY BRONTË

PUTTING DOWN THE CAT

The assistant holds her on the table,
the fur hanging limp from her tiny skeleton,
and the veterinarian raises the needle of fluid
which will put the line through her ninth life.

'Painless,' he reassures me, 'like counting
backwards from a hundred,' but I want to tell him
that our poor cat cannot count at all,
much less to a hundred, much less backwards.

ON THE DEATH OF A CAT

In life, death
was nothing
to you: I am

willing to wager
my soul that it
simply never occurred

to your nightmareless
mind, while sleep
was everything

(see it raised
to an infinite
power and perfection) – no death

in you then, so now
how even less. Dear stealth
of innocence

licked polished
to an evil
lustre, little

milk fang, whiskered
night
friend –

go.

From SONG FOR MOURNING A CAT

You became wild, you became a street cat!
Did you not fly around my heart like a nightingale?

No longer is your beauty a revelation,
Your face no longer a place of worship.

Your former tenderness grew coarse,
What were your fineries, became torn …

How can your beauty betray itself,
How can wine turn to quinine?

I'm afraid for you – decorated with jewelry –
And now you've become like a gypsy
prostituting herself.

An existentialist cat roaming the streets at night –
But who's still dreaming of you?

NIZAR QABBANI

From COLD MOUNTAIN POEMS

In other days, I was poor enough to suit,
But now I freeze in utter poverty:
I make the deal – it doesn't quite work out,
I take the road – it ends in misery;
I walk in the mud – my feet slip out from under,
I sit in the shrine – my belly gripes at me –
Since I lost the parti-colored cat,
Around the rice-jar, rats wait hungrily.

AN OFFERING FOR THE CAT

Since I got my cat Five White
the rats never bother my books.
This morning Five White died.
I make offerings of rice and fish,
bury you in mid-river
with incantations – I wouldn't slight you.
Once you caught a rat, ran round the garden with it
      squeaking in your mouth;
you hoped to put a scare into the other rats,
to clean up my house.
When we'd come aboard the boat
you shared our cabin
and though we'd nothing but meager dried rations,
we ate them without fear of rat piss and gnawing –
because you were diligent,
a good deal more so than the pigs and the chickens.
People make much of their prancing steeds;
They tell me nothing can compare to a horse or
      donkey –
Enough! – I'll argue the point no longer,
Only cry for you a little.

MEI YAO-CH'EN   225
TR. BRUNO WATSON

ON THE DEATH OF A CAT,
A FRIEND OF MINE AGED
TEN YEARS AND A HALF

Who shall tell the lady's grief
When her cat was past relief?
Who shall number the hot tears
Shed o'er her, belov'd for years?
Who shall say the dark dismay
Which her dying caused that day?

Come ye Muses, one and all,
Come obedient to my call;
Come and mourn with tuneful breath
Each one for a separate death;
And, while you in numbers sigh,
I will sing her elegy.

Of a noble race she came,
And Grimalkin was her name.
Young and old full many a mouse
Felt the prowess of her house;
Weak and strong full many a rat
Cowered beneath her crushing pat;
And the birds around the place
Shrank from her too-close embrace.

But one night, reft of her strength,
She lay down and died at length:
Lay a kitten by her side
In whose life the mother died.
Spare her life and lineage,
Guard her kitten's tender age,
And that kitten's name as wide
Shall be known as hers that died.
And whoever passes by
The poor grave where Puss doth lie,
Softly, softly let him tread,
Nor disturb her narrow bed.

From MATTHIAS

Rover, with the good brown head,
Great Atossa, they are dead;
Dead, and neither prose nor rhyme
Tells the praises of their prime.
Thou didst know them old and grey,
Know them in their sad decay.
Thou hast seen Atossa sage
Sit for hours beside thy cage;
Thou wouldst chirp, thou foolish bird,
Flutter, chirp – she never stirr'd!
What were now these toys to her?
Down she sank amid her fur;
Eyed thee with a soul resign'd –
And thou deemedst cats were kind!
– Cruel, but composed and bland,
Dumb, inscrutable and grand,
So Tiberius might have sat
Had Tiberius been a cat.

ODE ON THE DEATH OF A FAVOURITE CAT, DROWNED IN A TUB OF GOLDFISHES

'Twas on a lofty vase's side,
Where China's gayest art had dyed
   The azure flowers that blow;
Demurest of the tabby kind,
The pensive Selima, reclined,
   Gazed on the lake below.

Her conscious tail her joy declared;
The fair round face, the snowy beard,
   The velvet of her paws,
Her coat, that with the tortoise vies,
Her ears of jet, and emerald eyes.
   She saw, and purred applause.

Still had she gazed; but 'midst the tide
Two angel forms were seen to glide,
   The genii of the stream:
Their scaly armor's Tyrian hue
Through richest purple to the view
   Betrayed a golden gleam.

The hapless nymph with wonder saw:
A whisker first and then a claw,
  With many an ardent wish,
She stretched in vain to reach the prize.
What female heart can gold despise?
  What cat's averse to fish?

Presumptuous maid! with looks intent
Again she stretched, again she bent.
  Nor knew the gulf between.
(Malignant Fate sat by and smiled)
The slippery verge her feet beguiled,
  She tumbled headlong in.

Eight times emerging from the flood
She mewed to every watery god,
  Some speedy aid to send.
No dolphin came, no Nereid stirred;
Nor cruel Tom, nor Susan heard;
  A favourite has no friend!

From hence, ye beauties, undeceived,
Know, one false step is ne'er retrieved,
  And be with caution bold.
Not all that tempts your wandering eyes
And heedless hearts, is lawful prize;
  Nor all that glisters, gold.

LAST WORDS TO A
DUMB FRIEND

Pet was never mourned as you,
Purrer of the spotless hue,
Plumy tail, and wistful gaze,
While you humoured our queer ways,
Or outshrilled your morning call
Up the stairs and through the hall –
Foot suspended in its fall –
While, expectant, you would stand
Arched, to meet the stroking hand;
Till your way you chose to wend
Yonder, to your tragic end.

Never another pet for me!
Let your place all vacant be;
Better blankness day by day
Than companion torn away.
Better bid his memory fade,
Better blot each mark he made,
Selfishly escape distress
By contrived forgetfulness,
Than preserve his prints to make
Every morn and eve an ache.

From the chair whereon he sat
Sweep his fur, nor wince thereat;
Rake his little pathways out
Mid the bushes roundabout;
Smooth away his talons' mark
From the claw-worn pine-tree bark,
Where he climbed as dusk embrowned
Waiting us who loitered round.

Strange it is this speechless thing,
Subject to our mastering,
Subject for his life and food
To our gift, and time, and mood;
Timid pensioner of us Powers,
His existence ruled by ours,
Should – by crossing at a breath
Into safe and shielded death,
By the merely taking hence
Of his insignificance –
Loom as largened to the sense,
Shape as part, above man's will,
Of the Imperturbable.

As a prisoner, flight debarred,
Exercising in a yard,
Still retain I, troubled, shaken,
Mean estate, by him forsaken;

And this home, which scarcely took
Impress from his little look,
By his faring to the Dim,
Grows all eloquent of him.

Housemate, I can think you still
Bounding to the window-sill,
Over which I vaguely see
Your small mound beneath the tree,
Showing in the autumn shade
That you moulder where you played.

AS YOU WERE SAYING
for Richard Poirier

Telling me about Rosebud
(But not saying, 'put to sleep')
'A beautiful cat, so beautiful,
Even as she died,'
You say, on the phone,
And that was true, I had met her:
A lithe lovely shy tabby cat,
Hiding under the bedclothes, darting out.

But at that moment
As I listen, from California,
In the Truckee River I see two fat brown ducks,
Serene and elegant, and vastly silly.
How I wish you were here to come and look!
As they veer away from rocks
And sail downstream,
Like gamblers, headed for Reno.

From **CHANSONS INNOCENTES**

why did you go
little fourpaws?
you forgot to shut
your big eyes.

where did you go?
like little kittens
are all the leaves
which open in the rain.

little kittens who
are called spring,
is what we stroke
maybe asleep?

do you know? or maybe did
something go away
ever so quietly
when we weren't looking.

THE BLUE BOWL

Like primitives we buried the cat
with his bowl. Bare-handed
we scraped sand and gravel
back into the hole.
                    They fell with a hiss
and thud on his side,
on his long red fur, the white feathers
between his toes, and his
long, not to say aquiline, nose.

We stood and brushed each other off.
There are sorrows keener than these.

Silent the rest of the day, we worked,
ate, stared, and slept. It stormed
all night; now it clears, and a robin
burbles from a dripping bush
like the neighbor who means well
but always says the wrong thing.

THE EPITAPH OF FELIS

The Epitaph of Felis
Who departed this life in the year 1757, at the
    age of 14 years, 11 months and 4 days.

I most gentle of cats through long-drawn
        sickness aweary,
    Bidding a last farewell, turn to the waters below.
Quietly smiling to me says Queen Proserpina,
        'Welcome!
    Thine are the groves of the blest: thine the
        Elysian suns.'
If I deserve so well, O merciful Queen of the Silent,
    Let me come back one night, homeward
        returning again,
Crossing the threshold again in the ear of the master
        to murmur,
    'Even when over the Styx, Felis is faithful to thee.'

JOHN JORTIN   237
TR. SAMUEL COURTAULD

INDEX OF AUTHORS

240

ACKNOWLEDGMENTS

Thanks are due to the following copyright holders for permission to reprint:

GILLON AITKEN ASSOCIATES: 'This is My Chair' by Paul Gallico. Copyright © 1972 by Paul Gallico and Mathemata AG. Reprinted by permission of Gillon Aitken Associates. BEACON PRESS: 'Morning' by Mary Oliver. From *New and Selected Poems* by Mary Oliver. Copyright © 1992 by Mary Oliver. Reprinted by permission of Beacon Press, Boston. PROFESSOR ULLI BEIER: 'Song of the Lioness for her Cub'. Traditional African (Hottentot) chant. From *African Poetry: An Anthology of Traditional African Poems*, compiled and edited by Ulli Beier, Cambridge University Press. VINCENT BOURNE: 'Familiarity Dangerous' by William Cowper, translated from Latin by Vincent Bourne. Found in *101 Favourite Cat Poems*, compiled by Sara Whittier, Contemporary Books, 1991, Chicago. BRANDT AND HOCHMAN LITERARY AGENTS, INC.: 'Cat' from *The Skin Spinners* by Joan Aiken. Copyright © 1960, 1973, 1974, 1975, 1976 by Joan Aiken. Reprinted by permission of Brandt and Hochman Literary Agents, Inc. E. BRUCE BROOKS: 'Cold Mountain Poem #158' by Han Shan, translated by E. Bruce Brooks. Copyright E. Bruce Brooks. Reprinted by permission. CARCANET PRESS LIMITED: 'Poem (As the Cat)' and 'Young Cat and the Chrysanthemums' by William Carlos Williams, from *Collected Poems of William Carlos Williams*. Reprinted by permission of Carcanet Press Limited. CARLTON PUBLISHING GROUP: 'The Cat' by Ogden Nash, Carlton Publishing Group (André Deutsch). CITY LIGHTS BOOKS: 'Cat, you tumble down the street' by Fernando

247

Knopf, a division of Random House, Inc. 'The Cats of Greece' by Marge Piercy. From *Circles on the Water* by Marge Piercy, copyright © 1982 by Marge Piercy. Used by permission of Alfred A. Knopf, a division of Random House, Inc. CHANG-SOO KOH: 'The Spring is a Cat' by Jang-hi Lee, translated by Chang-soo Koh. Reprinted by permission of Chang-soo Koh. LIVERIGHT PUBLISHING CORPORATION: 'Chaplinesque' from *Complete Poems of Hart Crane* by Hart Crane, edited by Marc Simon. Copyright 1933, 1958, 1966 by Liveright Publishing Corporation. Copyright © 1986 by Marc Simon. Used by permission of Liveright Publishing Corporation. LOUISIANA STATE UNIVERSITY PRESS: 'The Cats of Balthus'. Reprinted by permission of Louisiana State University Press from *The Language Student* by Bin Ramke. Copyright © 1986 by Bin Ramke. JOHN MAJOR: 'Chang Tuan's Cats' by Wang Chih, translated by Felicity Bast, from *The Poetical Cat*, edited by John Major. Used by permission of John Major. MCCLELLAND & STEWART LTD: 'White Cat Blues' taken from *Angels of Flesh, Angels of Silence* by Lorna Crozier. Used by permission of McClelland & Stewart Ltd, The Canadian Publishers. HERBERT MITGANG: 'Nine Fat Cats in Little Italy' by Herbert Mitgang, from *Felines*, Chronicle Books, San Francisco. THE ESTATE OF HOWARD MOSS: 'Catsnip and Dogwood' by Howard Moss. NEW DIRECTIONS PUBLISHING CORPORATION: 'The Cat' by Lawrence Ferlinghetti, from *These are My Rivers*, copyright © 1993 by Lawrence Ferlinghetti. Reprinted by permission of New Directions Publishing Corp. 'Propriety' by Kawai Chigetsu-ni, translated by Kenneth Rexroth, from *Women Poets of Japan*, copyright © 1977 by Kenneth Rexroth and Ikuko Atsumi. Reprinted by permission of New Directions